Praise for *Leading with Questions*

"This book skillfully bridges scholarly theory and down-to-earth commonsense tactics to provide a crystal clear guide to a *very powerful* leadership technique that changes people and organizations."

> —Al D. McCready, chairman and CEO, McCready Manigold Ray & Co., Inc.

"*Leading with Questions* describes a very powerful and practical tool that has taken Constellation Power Generation into the top ranks of energy companies world wide."

> —Frank Andracchi, vice president, Constellation Energy Group

"Successful questioning is one of the most powerful skills not just for leaders but for all people, and Mike has spent his career both studying the power of questions and asking questions effectively. This book captures the wisdom of his experiences."

> —Keith M. Halperin, senior vice president, Personnel Decisions International

"I have experienced the tools and techniques of *Leading with Questions* firsthand and highly recommend this book to new as well as experienced leaders. It has dramatically changed our leaders as they learn how to embrace Marquardt's questioning technique."

> —Liz Cicco, training and development specialist, Bowne & Co., Inc.

"From the days of Socrates, our ability to ask the right questions has been revered as one of the greatest skills a person should possess when leading others. Marquardt's latest book is an invaluable 'how-to' resource for those intent upon finding solutions through reflective questioning."

> —Eric Charoux, executive director, DCDM Business School MAURITIUS

"*Leading with Questions* is brilliant and thought provoking. It is a huge wake-up call to all leaders that smarter questions are the best recipe for lasting success."

—Alastair Rylatt, author, *Winning the Knowledge Game: Smarter Learning for Business Excellence* and *Navigating the Frenzied World of Work*

"This book is a terrific guide and magnificent resource for those who wish to explore the power and benefits of leading with questions!"

—Dan Navarro, Quality Management Office, JPMorgan Chase Vastera

"*Leading with Questions* provides wonderful illumination on a subject often hidden in the shadows. In this book the genius of the author is his ability to capture the essence of what successful leaders do with questioning and how they can use questions to change their lives and those around them for the better."

—Kenneth L. Murrell, professor of management and MIS, The University of West Florida, and author, *Empowering Employees*

"The ability to frame and ask the right question is a desired skill for everyone in life. *Leading with Questions* is a must-read book for those engaged in developing people to their maximum potential."

—Mohammed Effendy Rajab, director, Adult Resources, World Organization of the Scout Movement, World Scout Bureau, Geneva

"Marquardt has powerfully expressed how to reach the heart of effective leadership. This is a book not just to enhance existing leadership power but to develop everyone's latent leadership qualities."

—Francesco Sofo, University of Canberra, Australia, and author, *Six Myths of Critical Thinking*

"Marquardt has discovered the way to effectively lead the twenty-first century organization through questions and reflective learning. This book captures the essence of the questioning process and sets a practical basis for the long-sought-after learning organization!"

—Harry Lenderman, president, The Elk Forge Group; advisor, Sodexho University; and author, *Breaking the Educational Glass Ceiling*

"By focusing on the right questions, Mike Marquardt has peeled back the onion to reveal the true power of questions. This book shows leaders how to give their organizations the cutting edge that makes the difference between a good company and a great company."

—Bea Carson, president, Carson Consulting

"The ideas in *Leading with Questions* will provide leaders with new perspective on leading in the challenging twenty-first century."

—Lim Peng Soon, president, Learning & Performance Systems

"This is a must-read book! *Leading with Questions* will change the way you manage in your organization. This book is Marquardt's latest contribution to improving the way we work and communicate in our increasingly complicated world."

—Howard Schuman, human resources advisor, Central Bank of Sri Lanka

"This book is the ideal guide for the corporate executive who would like to create a winning organization by asking the great questions."

—James Y. Lim, human resource manager, Alstom Corporation

"Leaders worldwide will be especially well served to master Marquardt's art of leading with questions!"

—Banu Golesorkhi, director, Research and Development, Pharos International

Leading with Questions

How Leaders Find the Right Solutions by Knowing What to Ask

Michael Marquardt

JOSSEY-BASS
A Wiley Imprint
www.josseybass.com

Published by Jossey-Bass
A Wiley Imprint
989 Market Street, San Francisco, CA 94103-1741   www.josseybass.com

Readers should be aware that Internet Web sites offered as citations and/or sources for further information may have changed or disappeared between the time this was written and when it is read.

Jossey-Bass books and products are available through most bookstores. To contact Jossey-Bass directly call our Customer Care Department within the U.S. at 800-956-7739, outside the U.S. at 317-572-3986, or fax 317-572-4002.

Jossey-Bass also publishes its books in a variety of electronic formats. Some content that appears in print may not be available in electronic books.

Library of Congress Cataloging-in-Publication Data
Marquardt, Michael J.
  Leading with questions : how leaders find the right solutions by knowing what to ask / by Michael Marquardt.—1st ed.
    p. cm.
  Includes bibliographical references and index.
  ISBN-13: 978-0-7879-7746-7 (alk. paper)
  ISBN-10: 0-7879-7746-2 (alk. paper)
  1. Leadership. 2. Communication in management. 3. Questioning. I. Title.
  HD57.7.M3924 2005
  658.4'5—dc22

                                                        2005015657

Printed in the United States of America
FIRST EDITION
HB Printing   10 9 8 7 6 5 4 3 2 1

Contents

INTRODUCTION

Do you feel that people aren't providing the information you need? Do you wonder whether the people in your organization really understand your vision for where things need to go? Do you speculate about what your boss is really thinking?

Have you ever thought about getting all this information, and more, by asking questions?

Questions can elicit information, of course, but they can do much more. Astute leaders use questions to encourage full participation and teamwork, to spur innovation and outside-the-box thinking, to empower others, to build relationships with customers, to solve problems, and more. Recent research—and the experience of a growing number of organizations—now points to the conclusion that the most successful leaders lead with questions, and they use questions more frequently. Successful and effective leaders create the conditions and environment to ask and be asked questions. When the Center for Creative Leadership studied 191 successful executives, its researchers discovered that the key to the executives' success was creating opportunities to ask, and then asking questions (Daudelin, 1996).

Consider these comments from among the successful leaders interviewed for this book:

- *Chad Holliday, chairman of the board and CEO of DuPont:* "I find that when someone engages me in a question, it wakes me up. I'm in different place. Throughout the day, I try to do the same thing. I ask questions: I rarely make statements until I have sized up the person's energy and focus, and whether they are open-minded; only then can I move. If I don't ask questions, I could be underrating the situation and problem, and miss the key issues."

- *Pentti Sydanmaanlakka, former director of human resources at Nokia Networks:* "Leading with questions has been always part of my leadership because I believe that leadership is not telling, but inspiring and showing others new places where they haven't been earlier."

- *Isabel Rimanoczy, partner, Leadership in International Management:* "I was working with pragmatic engineers who initially were upset that they were not able to get immediate answers and solutions to their questions. By focusing on questions rather than on answers, we inverted the process they were accustomed to. We put the focus on them, trusting their knowledge and wisdom. And, even when they did not think they had answers, they dived into themselves for the answers—and not surprisingly—they always found the answers. . . . They had increased their self-awareness and realized that there was wisdom inside them that could be unearthed with questions."

- *Robert Hoffman, executive director for organization development at Novartis:* "Questions have changed me immensely. I have greater self-confidence and a more relaxed attitude. I don't feel that I always have to have the answers in conversations or in situations where I need to speak at the spur of the moment. I feel this has increased my communications skills, especially listening and persuading."

These leaders have discovered the amazing power of questions. Questions wake people up. They prompt new ideas. They show people new places, new ways of doing things. They help us admit that we don't know all the answers. They help us become more confident communicators. Unfortunately, many leaders are unaware of the amazing power of questions, and how they can generate short-term results and long-term learning and success. If you have never considered making questions a tool in your leadership kit, this book is for you.

Of course, many leaders do ask questions constantly—questions such as these:

- Why are you behind schedule?
- Who isn't keeping up?
- What's the problem with this project?
- Whose idea was that?

Too often, we ask questions that disempower rather than empower our subordinates. These questions cast blame; they are not genuine requests for information.

Other sorts of questions are often no more than thinly veiled attempts at manipulation: *Don't you agree with me on that? Aren't you a team player?* If you tend to ask these sorts of questions, this book is for you.

So the point isn't that leaders just don't ask enough questions. Often, we don't ask the right questions. Or we don't ask questions in a way that will lead to honest and informative answers. Many of us don't know how to listen effectively to answers to questions—and haven't established a climate in which asking questions is encouraged.

And that's where this book comes in. The purpose of *Leading with Questions* is to help you become a stronger leader by learning how to ask the right questions effectively, how to listen effectively, and how to create a climate in which asking questions becomes as natural as breathing.

Research on Leaders Who Lead with Questions

Over the past twenty-five years, I have been involved in research and developing leaders around the world, both as a professor and as a consultant and adviser to corporate executives. I have noted more and more frequently that leaders of the more successful companies tended to question others and themselves more often. I have sought to discover why questions are so important to leaders, why they result in such success, and what questions are the most powerful and used most frequently.

Who are some of the leaders who ask questions? And when and why did these leaders first begin using questions in their leadership work? What questions did they find to have been most powerful and successful? Why do these leaders ask questions and what has been the impact of those questions on them and their organization? Over the past several years, I have asked individuals and audiences from around the world to identify leaders they believe use questions effectively. I then contacted professional colleagues who worked with leaders worldwide to identify leaders who both asked lots of questions in their work and were seen as successful leaders by their colleagues and subordinates. Occasionally the leaders I interviewed would refer me to another leader whom they saw as someone who also led with questions. I made an effort to get leaders from large and small companies, from public and private organizations, and from all parts of the world.

Among the many leaders that were identified, I interviewed a total of twenty-two leaders from all over the world. I prepared a list of questions that I would use in my interviews as follows:

- When did you start using questions and why?
- What are some of the ways in which you use questions?
- What questions have been most effective?
- What has been the impact of leading through questions on (a) your organization and (b) you as a leader?
- How has the use of questions changed you as a leader?

Their responses to these questions and their stories are interwoven throughout this book.

Throughout the pages of this book, you will find the experiences and questions asked by leaders who lead with questions.

Among those who shared their experiences as questioning leaders are CEOs and top leaders from DuPont, Alcoa, Novartis, and Cargill; public leaders from global and national agencies; academic leaders at the secondary and college levels. They come from Brazil, Finland, Malaysia, Mauritius, Korea, and Switzerland as well as North America. Brief biographies of these leaders are contained in Resource B.

Based on my quarter-century of experiences and interviews with scores of leaders who do indeed lead with questions, *Leading with Questions* provides a comprehensive foundation on ways to employ questions effectively when leading others. The book offers a variety of principles and strategies for asking questions as well as numerous stories of how leaders from every type of organization have used questions to attain organizational success and personal fulfillment.

Key Aspects of Leading with Questions

This book is composed of three parts. In Part One, I explain why questions can be so powerful for individuals and organizations. Chapter One examines why leaders often prefer to provide answers rather than ask questions and how limiting—and disastrous—that can be. I show why questioning is actually the ultimate leadership tool. Chapter Two details the benefits for leaders and organizations of creating a question-friendly organizational culture. A questioning culture strengthens individual and organizational learning; it improves decision making, problem solving, and teamwork, promotes adaptability and acceptance of change, and helps empower people by strengthening self-awareness and self-confidence.

Part Two offers practical guidance on asking questions effectively. Chapter Three explains the stumbling blocks many of us face in asking questions and tells the stories of several leaders who have overcome them and benefited enormously. Chapter Four shows how effective questions are empowering while ineffective questions disempower. It offers a thorough analysis of different types of questions, and it describes the roots of great questions. Chapter Five explores the art of asking questions effectively, examining how one's attitude, mindset, pace, and timing all affect the impact of asking questions. As this chapter demonstrates, active listening and following up are integral parts of the art of asking questions. Chapter Six turns from the personal level to the organizational, offering detailed advice on fostering an organizational culture that is conducive to questions.

Part Three presents guidelines for leaders on using questions to achieve specific results for individuals, teams, and organizations. Chapter Seven discusses how leaders can use questions in managing their staff, strengthening relationships with direct reports, helping them to grow and encouraging action and innovative thinking. This chapter also reviews the use of questions in orienting new staff, setting goals and objectives, conducting performance appraisals, and leading staff meetings, among other topics. Chapter Eight describes how leaders can use questions to improve team functioning, energize team meetings, solve problems, help teams overcome obstacles, and resolve conflict. Chapter Nine shows how questioning can strengthen entire organizations—sharpening strategy, vision, and values and building the capacity for change—focusing on questions with both internal and external stakeholder groups. The Conclusion encourages the reader to begin the journey to becoming a questioning leader.

Two resources are included in the book. Resource A describes two types of training programs to help leaders adopt questioning as an everyday tool of leadership. Resource B provides brief biographies of the leaders who participated in my research.

A New Level of Leadership

Leaders who lead with questions will create a more humane workplace as well as a more successful business. Leaders who use questions can truly empower people and change organizations. Most leaders are unaware of the potential of questions and needlessly endure a fractious, pressure-filled existence. My hope is that readers will change their style of leading and be more easily successful and fulfilled as leaders.

Without question, all of us, especially those of us who are leaders, need to ask more questions—questions that will assist in the development of individuals, teams, organizations, and ourselves. Questions have become essential for our success. Poor leaders rarely ask questions of themselves or others. Good leaders, on the other hand, ask many questions. Great leaders ask the great questions.

Part One

THE POWER OF QUESTIONS

1

AN UNDERUSED
MANAGEMENT TOOL

We live in a fast-paced, demanding, results-oriented world. New technologies place vast quantities of information at our fingertips in nanoseconds. We want problems solved instantly, results yesterday, answers immediately. We are exhorted to forget "ready, aim, fire" and to shoot now and shoot again. Leaders are expected to be decisive, bold, charismatic, and visionary—to know all the answers even before others have thought of the questions.

Ironically, if we respond to these pressures—or believe the hype about visionary leaders so prominent in the business press—we risk sacrificing the very thing we need to lead effectively. When the people around us clamor for fast answers—sometimes any answer— we need to be able to resist the impulse to provide solutions and learn instead to ask questions. Most leaders are unaware of the amazing power of questions, how they can generate short-term results and long-term learning and success. The problem is that we feel that we are supposed to have answers, not questions. I interviewed leaders around the world about their use—or avoidance— of questions. This comment by Gidget Hopf, president and CEO of Association for the Blind and Visually Impaired—Goodwill Industries, is typical: "I just automatically assumed that if someone was at my door with a problem, they expected me to solve it." Hopf thought it was her job to provide answers. Then she realized that there was another way:

Through coaching I realized how disempowering this is, and how much more effective I could be by posing the question back to the individual with the problem. . . . What I came to realize is that solving others' problems is exhausting. It is much more effective to provide the opportunity for them to solve their own problems.

Unfortunately, from an early age, we are discouraged from asking questions, especially challenging ones, be it at home, school, or at church, as they are considered rude, inconsiderate, or intrusive. Thus we become fearful of asking any questions. As we ask fewer questions, we become ever less comfortable and competent in asking questions.

And then when we become leaders, we feel that it is important for us to have answers rather than questions. Asking questions—or being unable to answer questions addressed to us—may show that we are somehow lacking as leaders. But this attitude leads to inertia. Consider what Jeff Carew, a vice president at Collectcorp, told me. "The easy way to lead, particularly if you are competent at your job, is to tell people how to do things in the way you have been successful." Usually, as Jeff has observed, people become successful either through a very capable boss who taught them the ropes or through their experiential learning that resulted in a successful track record and steady career advancement. Successful executives think they know the answers. "The problem with this is," Jeff noted, "if you do not create and maintain a working environment where you are always asking questions of your employees and forcing them to think, then you will probably never be any better tomorrow than you are today. Yesterday's solutions will not solve tomorrow's problems. I learned that you need to get to a different level of thinking if you are going to tackle tomorrow's problems— and who else is better to teach you how your environment is changing than the managers on the floor or in the trenches?"

Like Jeff Carew, a growing number of leaders recognize that their organization's success, if not survival, depends upon creating a learning organization, an organization that is able to quickly adapt to the changing environment, where every engagement becomes a learning opportunity, where learning and business objectives are necessarily interlinked. The ability to ask questions goes hand in hand with the ability to learn. A learning organization is only possible if it has a culture that encourages questions.

Do you ever feel defensive when people ask you questions? Do you ever hesitate to ask a question, fearing it may reveal ignorance or doubt? If so, you are closing off the free flow of information and ideas your organization needs and potentially undermining relationships with those around you. In fact, avoiding questions can cause serious harm, even disaster.

What Happens When Leaders Do Not Ask Questions

History is replete with tales of dire consequences experienced by leaders who did not ask questions. Recent disasters at the *New York Times*, Enron, and Arthur Anderson can be attributed to the lack of inquiring leaders. Historians who carefully examined the events and details behind the disasters of the *Titanic*, the *Challenger*, and the Bay of Pigs have determined a common thread—the inability or unwillingness of participants and leaders to raise questions about their concerns. Some group members were fearful that they were the only one who had a particular concern (when, in fact, it was later discovered that many people in the group had similar concerns). Others felt that their question had already been answered in the minds of other group members, and if they asked the question, it would be considered a dumb question; and they would be put down as being stupid or not going along with the group. Because people did not ask questions, people lost lives when the *Titanic* sank, when the *Challenger* crashed, when President Kennedy authorized a covert attack on the Bay of Pigs in Cuba.

Sinking of the *Titanic*

Why did the *Titanic* sink? When the luxury ship went down, on April 14, 1912, more than fourteen hundred passengers perished. Afterward, many questions were raised on both sides of the Atlantic. How could the allegedly unsinkable ship go down on its maiden voyage across the North Atlantic? What had gone wrong? Why couldn't the planner and builders have foreseen such a tragedy? Upon investigation, it was discovered that several of the planners and builders of the ship had indeed been concerned, though none of them had ever raised their concerns in the company of their colleagues. Why not? Because of their fear of appearing foolish by asking dumb questions. If no other "expert" seemed unsure about the structure and safety of the ship, then everything must be OK. Once the voyage was under way, many reports came in from nearby ships describing icebergs around them. "*Titanic* received many incoming messages warning of ice," Robert E. Mittelstaedt writes in *Will Your Next Mistake Be Fatal?* (2005, p. 101), "but there is no mention of her inquiring of others for updates or more information. What if someone was curious enough to ask for more information from the ships in the area?"

The Explosion of the *Challenger* Spacecraft

The spacecraft was launched on January 28, 1986, and exploded seventy-three seconds after liftoff. Much of the research into what went wrong with the *Challenger* launch focuses on the lack of communication between NASA, Morton Thiokol, Inc. (MTI) and the Marshall Space Center. MTI was the contractor responsible for the component that failed during the launch and depended on Marshall for the contract, and Marshall depended on NASA for funding and support. Almost two years before the fatal launch, MTI became aware that there could be a problem with the O-ring, a sealing component that prevents hot gases from escaping the solid rocket booster and burning a hole in the fuel tank (the physical cause of the *Challenger* disaster). The engineers at MTI documented this problem and insisted that further testing needed to be done to determine the reliability of the O-ring. Upon further testing they confirmed that the O-ring *was not* reliable, particularly when temperatures dropped below fifty-three degrees. Why then was the *Challenger* given the go to launch on January 28, 1986, when the temperature at launch time was thirty-six degrees, well below the safety margin? The people around the table were afraid to express their doubts or even to ask questions that they had determined before entering the room that morning that they would ask.

The 1961 Bay of Pigs Invasion

Fears of shattering the warm feelings of perceived unanimity—of rocking the boat—kept some of Kennedy's advisers from objecting to the Bay of Pigs plan before it was too late. "How could I have been so stupid?" President John F. Kennedy asked after the Bay of Pigs fiasco. What happened? In 1961, CIA and military leaders wanted to use Cuban exiles to overthrow Fidel Castro. After lengthy consideration among his top advisers, Kennedy approved a covert invasion. Advance press reports alerted Castro to the threat. More than fourteen hundred invaders arrived at the *Bahía de Cochinos* (Bay of Pigs) to find themselves vastly outnumbered. Lacking air support, necessary ammunition, and an escape route, nearly twelve hundred surrendered. Others died. Top CIA leaders blamed Kennedy for not authorizing vital air strikes. Other CIA analysts fault the wishful thinking that the invasion would stimulate an uprising among Cuba's populace and military. Planners assumed the invaders could simply fade into the mountains for guerilla operations. Trouble was, eighty miles of swampland separated the bay from the mountains. The list goes on. *Groupthink* was the term Irving Janis (1971) chose to use for the phenomenon: the kind of flawed group dynamics that lets bad ideas go unchallenged by questions and disagreement and can sometimes yield disastrous outcomes. Kennedy's top advisers were unwilling to challenge bad ideas because it might disturb perceived or desired group concurrence. Presidential adviser Arthur Schlesinger, for instance, presented serious objections to the invasion in a memorandum to the president, but suppressed his doubts at the team meetings. Attorney General Robert Kennedy privately admonished Schlesinger to support the president's decision to invade. At one crucial meeting, JFK called on each member for his vote for or against the invasion. Each member, that is, except Schlesinger—whom he knew to have serious concerns. Many members assumed other members agreed with the invasion plan. Schlesinger later lamented, "In the months after the Bay of Pigs I bitterly reproached myself for having kept so silent during those crucial discussions in the cabinet room." He continued, "I can only explain my failure to do more than raise a few timid questions by reporting that one's impulse to blow the whistle on this nonsense was simply undone by our inability to challenge one another and ask questions" (Janis, 1971, p. 76). After that huge blunder, JFK revamped his decision-making process to encourage questions, dissent, and critical evaluation among his team.

Day-to-Day Disaster Prevention

Questions and a questioning attitude are not just important for avoiding historic disasters: they are also useful day in and day out for giving feedback, problem solving, strategic planning, resolving conflicts, team building, and more. When we avoid questions, all these activities suffer, even if they don't lead to disasters of historic proportions. Consider what Cindy Stewart, president and CEO of the Family Health Council of Central Pennsylvania, told me:

> One of the first jobs that I had was in a sewing factory. My job title was "floor girl," which was the assistant to the "floor lady"—no kidding! This job entitled moving work from one process to another to assure that none of the workers in your section were without work, and that specific garment lots would be completed by the deliverable date. It was not considered a management position. I distinctly remember overhearing the management team discussing a particular bottleneck that routinely occurred with this one style of nightgown. As they wrestled with solutions, none of which worked, I can clearly recall that I was thinking, "I wish they would ask me." Since I was the one that worked the closest to the problematic process, I felt I was in the best position to solve the problem. Of course, they never did ask me.

In avoiding questions, the management team at that sewing factory closed off a potentially important source of ideas and information, and their problem-solving ability suffered as a result. The experience left a lasting impression on Stewart.

> I think I made up my mind at that time that, if I were ever to be in a leadership position, I would never assume that having the title would mean that I had all the answers. Over my twenty-plus years in executive positions, I have come to realize that much of my success can be attributed to the fact that I believe in the capacity of the people who have worked with me. I truly think that the leader who tries to know it all and tells everyone what to do is doomed to failure.

Facing Reality

No company can become great, Jim Collins tells us in *Good to Great*, without the ability to confront the "brutal facts of reality" (2001, p. 88). Consider the story of the Boston Red Sox. The team's recent World Series win, as is well known, was long in coming. But in the 1940s the Red Sox was one of the dominant teams in baseball. Then in the 1950s the team went into a significant decline. One reason for the decline was attributed to racism. As other major league teams were widening their talent pools by recruiting black players, the Red Sox was slow to change. It passed on hiring Jackie Robinson and Willie Mays, and became the last major league team to recruit black players. Not until 1959 did a black player show up on the diamond in a Red Sox uniform. Prejudice played an obvious role. But reinforcing this prejudice was an unquestioning attitude. As Sidney Finkelstein writes in *Why Smart Executives Fail*, "Tom Yawkey, the owner of the Boston Red Sox, provides an all-too-typical example [of complacent prejudice]. When his scouts reported that African-American players were not good enough or simply not ready for big league play, he accepted their reports without question. Yet any serious attempt to verify these evaluations might have caused Yawkey to question his picture of baseball reality" (2003, p. 200). When leaders fail to ask questions, they forgo the opportunity to test their own assumptions and prejudices, whether those prejudices involve race or beliefs about consumer behavior, strategic threats, market conditions, product quality, staff abilities, or what have you.

The failure to ask questions, in other words, allows us to operate with a distorted sense of reality. In fact, Finkelstein calls companies that are unable to question their prevailing view of reality *zombies*. A zombie company, he says, is "a walking corpse that just doesn't yet know that it's dead—because this company has created an insulated culture that systematically excludes any information that could contradict its reigning picture of reality" (2004, p. 25). But as GE's former CEO Jack Welch says, leading successfully means, "seeing the world the way it is, not the way we hope it will be or wish it to be" (Tichy, 2002, p. 64). Those responsible for the Bay of Pigs, the *Challenger* disaster, and the sinking of the *Titanic* were all operating under a distorted picture of reality because they failed to ask questions.

Organizations and leaders that avoid questions are actually losing opportunities to learn, according to Noel Tichy. "This is not a trivial issue. Many executives close off learning. In their day-to-day interactions with staff they are usually either issuing instructions or making judgments about the ideas or performance of others" (2002, p. 60). By telling rather than asking, Tichy says, they are actually making their organizations dumber, "less smart, less aligned, and less energized every day." In such organizations, "there is little or no knowledge transfer, intelligence is assumed to reside at the top, and everyone below senior management is expected to check their brains at the door" (p. 53).

Mike Parker, president and CEO of Dow Chemical, notes, "a lot of bad leadership comes from an inability or unwillingness to ask questions. I have watched talented people—people with much higher IQs than mine—who have failed as leaders. They can talk brilliantly, with a great breadth of knowledge, but they're not very good at asking questions. So while they know a lot at a high level, they don't know what's going on way down in the system. Sometimes they are afraid of asking dumb questions, but what they don't realize is that the dumbest questions can be very powerful. They can unlock a conversation" (2001, p. 37).

Questions as the Ultimate Leadership Tool

Oakley and Krug (1991) call questions the "ultimate empowerment tool" for the leader. They observe that the better we as leaders become at asking effective questions and listening for the answers to those questions, the more consistently we and the people with whom we work can accomplish mutually satisfying objectives, be empowered, reduce resistance, and create a willingness to pursue innovative change.

John Kotter, the noted Harvard professor and author on leadership, writes that key difference between leaders and managers is that leaders focus on getting to the right questions whereas managers focus on finding solutions to those questions (1998). The focus on finding answers must not obscure the importance of asking the right questions. Successful leaders know that they cannot get the right answer without asking the right questions.

In a recent *Harvard Business Review* article, Peter Drucker (Drucker & Maciariello, 2004) writes that he found that effective executives all tended to follow the same nine practices:

- They asked, "What needs to be done?"
- They asked, "What is right for the enterprise?"
- They developed action plans.
- They took responsibility for decisions.
- They took responsibility for communicating.
- They were focused on opportunities rather than problems.
- They ran productive meetings.
- They thought and said "we" rather than "I."
- They listened first, spoke last!

Questions are at the heart of each of these practices.

The importance of asking questions was forcefully conveyed in 1843 when John Stuart Mill wrote *The System of Logic*, in which he noted the emptiness of a set of opinions accumulated without the help of strong-sense critical thinking. "He who knows only his side of the case knows little of that. His reasons may have been good, and no one may have been able to refute them. But if he is equally unable to refute the reasons on the opposite side, he has no ground or preferring with opinion."

The ability to ask questions effectively is one of a leader's most important tools. Donald Peterson, former CEO of Ford Motor Company, once remarked, "Asking more of the right questions reduces the need to have all the answers."

When Alan Wurtzel, as the new CEO of Circuit City, first began turning the company around, he started with the realization that he did not know what to do next. He resisted the urge to walk in with answers, and instead began with questions. According to Jim Collins (2001), Wurtzel stands as one of the few CEOs in a large corporation who really made use of questions, with both his top team and his board. Each step along the way, Wurtzel would keep asking questions until he had a clear picture of reality and its implications.

> When Alan Wurtzel started the long traverse from near bankruptcy to these stellar results, he began with a remarkable answer to the questions of where to take the company: *I don't know.* . . . Wurtzel resisted the urge to walk in with "the answer." Instead, once he had the right people on the bus, he began not with answers, but with *questions* [emphasis in original]. "Alan was a real spark," said a board member. "He had the ability to ask questions that were just marvelous. We had some wonderful debates in the board room. It was never just a dog and pony show, where you would just listen and then go to lunch." Indeed, Wurtzel stands as one of the few CEOs in a large corporation who put more questions to his board members than they put to him [Collins, 2001, pp. 74–75].

In my own interviews with successful leaders, I found a similar willingness to express ignorance and an equal respect for the power of questions. Consider these remarks from Douglas Eden, president of Cargill's Malt Americas division:

> When I came back from my assignments overseas and was appointed president of Malt Americas, I was asked to make critical changes as the business was failing. We had to quickly decide whether to stay in or exit, and if we stayed in, what changes would be necessary to make the business viable. I did not consciously make a decision to become a questioning leader, but it began to naturally occur as I had lots of questions and had to search for answers. Should we remain an efficient, low-cost supplier or should we become the premier solution provider to the brewery business? What would be of most value to brew masters? Technical solutions such as better foam and flavor, or supply chain solutions?
>
> I was new to the brewer's malt business and naturally had lots of questions. Some of the staff wanted me to be more directive, and to tell them how to execute various tasks. I really did not know immediately what to do, and was not ready to immediately propose strategies. Some were more comfortable with this approach than others. As we all got better at asking questions of each other, we generated solutions that led to longer-term contracts and more value to our customers.
>
> Now, four years later, we are a more successful business. I attribute much of this success to our ability to ask questions. Our business is very complex, and we have to search for the answers together.

Both these leaders were willing to say "I don't know" and to ask questions and work with others to find answers. As Collins tells us, "Leading from good to great does not mean coming up with answers and then motivating everyone to follow your messianic vision. It means having the humility to grasp the fact that you do not yet understand enough to have the answers and then to ask the questions that will lead to the best possible insights" (2001, p. 75).

Another example of a leader who makes effective use of questions is Commander D. Michael Abrashoff. Through what he calls "Grassroots Leadership," Commander Abrashoff turned around the operations of the USS *Benfold*, one of the U.S. Navy's most modern warships. His methods were not complex, yet the results were astounding. Under Abrashoff's twenty-month command, the *Benfold* operated on 75 percent of its allocated budget, returning $1.4 million to the Navy coffers. During that time, the ship's combat readiness indicators were the highest ever in the history of the Pacific Fleet. The promotion rate of his people was two and a half times the Navy average. The predeployment training cycle, which usually takes a total of fifty-two days, was completed by the *Benfold* crew in just nineteen days. During a twelve-month period under the previous command, there were twenty-eight disciplinary actions for which twenty-three sailors were discharged. During Abrashoff's tenure there were five disciplinary cases and no discharges. Under his predecessor thirty-one people were detached from the ship for limited duty, usually for complaints of bad backs. He had only two crew members leave for health reasons. A third of all recruits don't make it through their first term of enlistment, and only 54 percent of sailors stay in the Navy after their second duty tour. Commander Abrashoff had 100 percent of the *Benfold*'s career sailors signing on for another tour. It is estimated that this retention alone saved the Navy $1.6 million in 1998 (Crowley, 2004).

What did he do to stage such a turnaround in less than twenty months? As he himself remarks, he continuously asked questions; he listened, and then he acted on what he heard. Almost immediately upon taking command, he had a fifteen- to twenty-minute personal interview with each of his staff of three hundred. He asked each person these three questions: "What do you like best about this ship? What do you like least? What would you change if you could?"

Abrashoff acted as quickly as he could to implement the ideas that came from these questions. He realized that simply following existing procedures and doing things the way they had always been done could no longer be effective.

Abrashoff set the vision and trusted his crew. He helped people take pride in their work.

> Whenever I didn't get the results I was looking for on the *Benfold*, I tried to look inward before flying off the handle. I also asked myself three questions each time: Did I clearly articulate the goals I was try-ing to achieve? Did I give people the time and resources they needed to succeed? Did I give them enough training to get the job done properly?" Eighty percent of the time, I found that I was part of the problem and that, through my actions alone, I could have altered the outcome significantly.

Abrashoff questioned every rule. He noted that when an officer or sailor came to him for approval or a signature on something, his first question was always, "Why do we do it this way?"

> If the answer was, "Because this is the way it's always been done," I would say, "That's not good enough. Find out if there is a better way to do this."
>
> After a while, people began doing their homework before they ever brought issues to me. And they could explain, "This is why we do things this way." Or, "We've thought of a better way to get this accomplished." It drove my officers crazy, but by creating a culture in which we questioned everything, we were training our people to keep their eyes open to new ways of doing business [Abrashoff, 2002].

Great Questions Define Great Leaders

Asking rather than telling, questions rather than answers, has become the key to leadership excellence and success in the twenty-first century. Peter Drucker, considered the leadership guru of the twentieth century and still going strong, notes that the leader of the past may have been a person who knew how to tell, but certainly the leader of the future will be a person who knows how to ask. With the growing complexity and speed of change in the world, the traditional hierarchical model of leadership that worked yesterday will not work tomorrow. The leader simply won't know enough to adequately tell people what to do; the world is changing too rapidly. No one person can master all the data needed to address the complex issues that confront today's organizations.

Michael Dell, founder and leader of the computer company that bears his name, is a strong believer in the power of questions. "Asking lots of questions opens new doors to new ideas, which ultimately contributes to your competitive edge," he says (Tichy, 2002, p. 61). Dell is also a big believer in learning from everyone in the company. It does this systematically by polling people around the company. "We also learn a lot by asking the same question in similar groups across the company and comparing the results. . . . If one team is having great success with medium-sized companies, we cross-pollinate their ideas . . . throughout the organization."

Leaders need to create a questioning climate where employees feel safe and able to trust the system and the people involved. Without this level of safety and comfort, people are generally unwilling to be vulnerable, and to be comfortable answering questions that might seem threatening. And without trust and openness, people are unwilling to communicate about feelings and about problems, and thus ask the leader questions that may help them.

Marshall Goldsmith, recognized as one of the top leadership coaches, regularly teaches leaders to ask questions. In "Ask, Learn, Follow Up and Grow," he writes,

> The effective leader of the future will consistently ask—to receive advice and to solicit new ideas. Tomorrow's leader will ask a variety of key stakeholders for ideas, opinions, and suggestions. Vital sources of information will include present and potential customers, suppliers, team members, cross-divisional peers, direct reports, managers, other members of the organization, researchers, and thought leaders. The leader will ask in a variety of ways: through leadership inventories,

satisfaction surveys, phone calls, voice mail, e-mail, the Internet, satellite hookups, and in-person dialogue [1996, pp. 229–230].

Aside from the obvious benefit of gaining new ideas and insights, Goldsmith adds, "asking by top leaders has a secondary benefit that may be even more important. The leader who asks is providing a role model. Sincere asking demonstrates a willingness to learn, a desire to serve, and a humility that can be an inspiration for the entire organization" (p. 231).

Looking Ahead

Contrary to much received wisdom, effective leaders do not have all the answers. Instead, effective leaders make it a practice to ask questions. One of the best things you can do to strengthen your leadership is to ask questions. Another is to encourage others to ask questions.

When we learn to ask questions, and do so effectively, our questions can transform individuals, groups, and organizations. How this is so is the topic of the next chapter, which explains the many dividends that a question-friendly organizational culture pays.

2

BENEFITS OF A QUESTIONING CULTURE

We have all heard sayings like these:

Go along to get along.

Don't rock the boat.

They're not paying me enough to think.

If these and similar comments are commonplace around your organization, it is safe to say that it does not have a questioning culture. In organizations that discourage questions, information is usually hoarded, people keep their heads down and stick to their knitting, and few people are willing to take any risks. In answer-driven organizations, curiosity, risk taking, challenging the status quo, and even the willingness to be wrong takes a back seat (Goldberg, 1998a). The prevailing culture of such organizations, either implicitly or explicitly, calls for rigidity, risk avoidance, protectiveness, defensiveness, and automatic routines and habits. These organizations usually suffer from low morale, poor teamwork, and poor leadership. They become fossilized, even moribund.

Leaders, through questions, can build a culture in which questions are welcomed, assumptions are challenged, and new ways to solve problems are explored. Questions establish an inquiring culture in organizations, and such an inquiring culture builds a learning organization. Michael Dell, founder of Dell Inc. observes that "Asking lots of questions opens new doors to new ideas, which ultimately contributes to your competitive edge. . . . That's why you must encourage the free flow of information at all levels" (Tichy, 2002, p. 61).

Questions also build a culture of accountability. They can foster commitment without barter and sustain the corporate community through civic engagement (Block, 2003). Jack Welch, in his recent book *Winning* (2005), states that leaders must be the ones who indeed ask the most and the best questions.

What Is a Questioning Culture?

When we ask questions of others and invite them to search for answers with us, we are not just sharing information, we are sharing responsibility. A questioning culture is a culture in which responsibility is shared. And when responsibility is shared, ideas are shared, problems are shared (problems are not yours or mine, but *ours*), and ownership of results is shared. When an organization develops a questioning culture, it also creates a culture of *we*, rather than a culture of you versus me, or management versus employees.

Pentti Sydanmaanlakka, a former HR director at Nokia, outlines some of the qualities that a questioning culture generates:

> Leading with questions gives the opportunity for the subordinates to be more active. To be active, they need to learn the skill of self-leadership. Through questions, they will also take more responsibility and be more motivated and committed. People like the feeling that they have found the answer themselves. Leading with questions means that there is an atmosphere where you can challenge everything; questions create an open communications culture. Leading with questions for me personally has meant more freedom as a boss.

Kouzes and Posner emphasize the importance of leaders' engaging people throughout the organization in what they do and why they do it. They ask us to imagine how much more ownership of the values of the organization there would be when leaders actively involve a wide range of people in their development. "Shared values," they note, "are the result of listening, appreciating, building consensus and practicing conflict resolution. For people to understand the values and come to agree with them, they must participate in the process. Unity is forged, not forced" (2002, p. 83).

Questions asked by leaders transform the organization as they can evoke the images of what employees hope to create, and of the values and behaviors desired by their people. Leaders show through the power of their questions and the words chosen within those questions the means as well as the metaphors for organizational vision, values, attitudes, behaviors, structures, and concepts.

A questioning culture has six hallmarks. When an organization has a questioning culture, the people in it

- Are willing to admit, "I don't know."
- Go beyond allowing questions; they encourage questions.
- Are helped to develop the skills needed to ask questions in a positive way.
- Focus on asking empowering questions and avoid disempowering questions.
- Emphasize the process of asking questions and searching for answers rather than finding the "right" answers.
- Accept and reward risk taking.

All these topics are discussed in this chapter or in subsequent chapters of the book.

Organizational Benefits of a Questioning Culture

Questions serve as the foundation for increasing individual, team, and organizational learning. Every question can be a potential learning opportunity. Education theorists (Bruner, 1974; Bandura, 1977; Knowes, Holton, & Swanson, 1998) note that deep and significant learning occurs only as a result of reflection, and reflection is not possible without a question—whether the question be from an external or internal source. A culture that encourages questions likewise encourages learning.

The act of questioning actually has a physiological impact on the human brain. The neurons make more connections because of the body's need to deal with a question. To demonstrate this, take a heading in this or any book and convert it into a question. For example, consider the statement "action learning helps us to learn." If you simply ask yourself "How does action learning help us to learn?" you will be surprised at how much more you will learn and retain of what you read in that section.

Learning depends upon curiosity and asking questions. The experience of curiosity is equivalent to continuously living and operating out of a question frame as simple as "what's this?" as all children do. It is through questions that we operationalize curiosity into behavior, and as a result they are the foundation of any kind of learning, be it formal, informal, or personal (Goldberg, 1998a, pp. 8–9). Questions, especially challenging ones, cause us to think and to learn.

Jeff Carew, vice president of Collectcorp, explains the role of questions in organizational learning:

> Collectcorp is becoming more of a classroom. . . . Our working environment is one in which everyone is asking questions on how to make things work better. We are not looking for "the answer," we are looking for better solutions than any one of us could come up with on our own.
>
> Yesterday's solutions will not solve tomorrow's problems. I learned that you need to get to a different level of thinking if you are going to tackle tomorrow's problems and who else is better to teach you how your environment is changing than the managers on the floor or in the trenches?

Carew highlights an important aspect of a questioning culture. A questioning culture promotes ongoing questions. The point is not to find the answer. Rather, in a questioning culture we keep asking and learning. We may come up with an answer today—and a better answer tomorrow. As Effendy Mohamed Rajab of the World Organization of the Scout Movement told me, "there is no such thing as the correct answer." Rajab says the point of asking questions is to gain perspective.

Mark Harper, president of Wholesale Marketing for ConocoPhillips Petroleum, stresses that gaining new perspectives is one of the most important uses of questions. He says he uses questions to encourage people "to see things from a different perspective." And he adds, "Surfacing and changing unconscious biases is very important." When we open our eyes and minds to the perspective of others, we open ourselves to learning.

Vance Coffman (2002), former chairman and CEO of Lockheed Martin, comments that he built a learning organization by asking questions. "Great questions are good fuel for fostering curiosity. Great questions guide my search for common sense explanations of a situation." When asked, *what critical questions should a new senior executive at Lockheed Martin ask*, he replied: Why is this the way it is? Do we understand why we got there?" He continued:

> Good questions make better programs or get us out of problems, whatever the circumstances are. If people on your team value what's important, why it's important, and what's the logic that drives us to do this versus that, then you've got a pretty good team. Once I'm comfortable with the way a team's decision process works and how the team members work together, that team will solve problems and deliver terrific results. But if a team isn't functioning well, I first ask why and then how can we change it to get better players in the right jobs at the right time. When the right players are in place, a solid team can be honest enough, curious enough, and interested enough to push each other on why our company is doing this, how it got there, and where it is going. Essentially, I want two sharpened edges in a team: critical inquiry combined with collaborative action [p. 39].

In fact inquiry and collaborative action naturally go together. It is hard to collaborate with others without asking and answering questions. And asking and answering questions in a positive way naturally leads to collaboration.

Improved Decision Making and Problem Solving

As a questioning culture promotes learning, it also helps improve decision making and problem solving. Questioning helps people gain perspective and understand the perspectives of others. As they see issues and problems from different points of view, they gain an appreciation for their complexity—and also expand the range of possible solutions. When I interviewed David Smyk, a partner with Executive Healthcare, he highlighted the value of perspective in decision making and problem solving:

> It has been my experience that people who are immersed in a project often do not readily see the possible solutions that lie beyond their comfort zone of knowledge. As a questioner, I can help increase their vision by challenging them to define issues in ways that are new to them. These generally open-ended questions are nonthreatening, and when a person does not feel they are "on the spot," the flow of creative thinking can be accelerated. In addition, the proper framing of questions makes it easy to view the questioner as a team member who can assist in achieving a successful outcome and not as an obstacle to the process.

Organizations that encourage leaders at all levels to take the time to ask thoughtful and probing questions improve the odds of making good decisions. When you talk to the people closest to the problem, you can gather more relevant information, gain a better perspective, and be able to act more confidently than if you relied solely on your own resources, opinions, and perceptions.

By their nature, questions help us to think clearly, logically, and strategically. Questions increase communications and listening as well as prevent us from misjudging each others' motivation. We can find the truth more easily through listening to each other's questions than being forced to listen to opinions and statements that are based on assumptions. Truth emerges not from opinions but from the free movement of open minds. Questioning causes us to view one another as resources.

Questions encourage and enable individuals and groups to understand, to clarify, and to open up new avenues of exploration for solving the problem. They provide new insights and ideas for strategic actions and potential paths for solutions. Questions and responses to those questions provide necessary and valuable information to solve problems faster and make better decisions. They provide leaders the opportunity to gain unfiltered information. Through questions, leaders seek to learn not only what directly causes the problem or what solutions may work (which is single-loop learning), but also to seek to discover and learn what might be the underlying causes and solutions (double-loop learning) as well as the culture and mindset that creates these causes and solutions (triple-loop learning).

Mark Harper of ConocoPhillips points to another benefit of a questioning culture. It helps create "a higher level of trust that dialogue and debate will occur before major decisions are made." As a result, he says, people feel included in the process and "there is more of a commitment to execution when changes have to be implemented."

Questions also generate alignment with a shared focus and make it more likely that you will solve the right problem. In *Smart Thinking for Crazy Times* (1998), Ian Mitroff observes that individuals and organizations run into trouble because they too often solve the wrong problem. Organizational psychologists such as Block (2003) and Vaill (1996) note that the problem originally presented is rarely the most critical problem for the group to work on; oftentimes it is only a symptom, and a more urgent and important problem emerges as the group works on it. Leaders thus need to recognize that problem solving begins by first diverging through the use of inquiry, and only then using questions that create the converging and narrowing focus.

Too often leaders assume that they have a clear picture of the problem. The obvious (but not always practiced) first step in solving any problem is first to be sure you know what the problem is. Most of us presuppose, because we have heard about or experienced the problem, that we now know and understand exactly what the problem is. And, even more dangerously, we believe everyone else now has the same perception and understanding of the problem. In reality, if seven people experience the same problem, they will probably come up with seven different descriptions of what the problem is.

A questioning culture helps to undercut these typical and erroneous assumptions. When questions are routine and habitual, different perspectives will be highlighted naturally, and a fuller picture of the problem will result. The group will be more able to gain the big-picture perspective of the problem and a fuller understanding of the entire range of possible solutions before determining goals and specific strategies. The acquisition of a wide, helicopter view of the problem can only be accomplished by openly and freshly questioning each other and then reflecting on the responses. A central aspect of the reflective inquiry process is to encourage people to ask dumb—or, more accurately, *fresh*—questions.

Greater Adaptability and Acceptance of Organizational Change

Change brings new ideas, new ways of doing things to the organization. Change and new ideas are often rejected in organizations without a questioning culture because they might conflict with existing, established mental models or ways of doing things, *which have never been questioned*. When questions are rare, those promoting new ideas have the task of confronting these existing assumptions without invoking defensiveness or anger. This is difficult to do in organizations where the prevailing culture discourages questions. Their questions, no matter how gently phrased, stand out and seem disruptive because questions are so rare. When an organization develops a questioning culture, however, questions cease to be unusual, cease to be threatening. This makes it easier for even difficult and challenging questions to be addressed—and for the organization to adapt to change.

When faced with change, people focus on what they are going to lose. The more people feel that they make a difference, the better they will feel about what they are doing. The better they feel about what they are doing, the more their self-esteem is enhanced and the more contributions they will make. By posing the right questions and engaging staff in the pursuit of a response, effective leaders gain more than just buy-in to the change. Effective leaders serve as the catalyst for change and give their followers the opportunity to exert some control in determining their future. Questions will enable staff to become more aware of how they contribute to the organization's goals, and thereby generate greater commitment to those goals.

Great questions cause the questioner to become more aware of the need for change, and to be more open and willing to change. The questions themselves may actually cause the leader to become a change catalyst. The leader who leads with questions will more likely champion new ideas heard and developed in the inquiry. New ideas and perspectives enable the leader to make strong arguments for advocating change.

Motivating and Empowering Employees

Good questions energize people. And a questioning culture can energize an entire organization. Margaret Wheatley (2002) notes how questions and the resulting reflection nourish people and develop internal motivation. Questions create the conditions that foster openness and release energy. People are energized when they are questioned, because they have been asked for their ideas.

"Asking questions is fun," Doug Eden says. "Employees enjoy it." Eden is president of Cargill's Malt Americas unit. He began his career with Cargill in 1978 as a staff accountant in Minneapolis and served in senior management positions in Thailand and Australia as well as eight cities in the United States before becoming president. Asking questions, he says, "leads to meaningful dialogue, gets everyone involved, and actually provides me more credibility as a leader."

Blanchard (2003) remarks that too many leaders try to make people feel unimportant. The important thing about leadership is not what happens when you're there but what happens when you are *not* there. Leaders who promote a questioning culture in their organizations move people from dependence to independence. Blanchard notes that great questions equip people so that positive things happen when you are not there. Questions create a supportive, creative environment. By asking questions, leaders help people discover for themselves what is important for them in doing what is necessary for the organization. This discovery process improves their self-confidence and self-esteem, empowering them in the process. Concurrently, they take ownership of the solution because they have participated in developing it.

Questions can certainly empower and motivate people more effectively than exhortatory statements do. When leaders encourage a questioning culture, they put out subtle messages that build their people's self-esteem and self-confidence, which is a key to shifting their thinking paradigm. This message—"I care about what you think, and your opinion is important and it counts around here"—motivates people and builds positive attitude as well as enhancing their personal satisfaction.

Good questions empower people to devise their own solutions. When people discover their own answers, they develop self-responsibility and accept ownership of the results. Asking people questions shows them that you value them. Questions move people from dependence to independence.

Stronger Teamwork

Putting people together around a conference table doesn't make them into a team whose members all pull together. Sue Whitt, global head of Pharmaceutical Regulatory Operations at Abbott Labs, previously served as senior vice president for Pfizer's global R&D business. She explained to me how she encouraged a questioning culture to bring her team together when she was at Pfizer:

> When I directed the integration for development operation at Pfizer, I had an integration team staffed with ten people from different

segments. Staff meetings used to be very "un-group-like." Everyone was constantly talking over each other, debating who's the smartest. It was difficult to get the group back to the goal of the meeting. Questions I asked began to change my group.

I would ask about data. "Are you aware of how many databases need to be done by the end of the year? Would you like to prioritize? If so, on what basis, and how should we reprioritize?" At the end of each session, we asked questions such as, "What worked and what went well? What could we do better?" We would then be sure to incorporate these ideas into our next session. I have continued to use this approach in my group meetings.

The people on any team possess an array of knowledge, wisdom, creativity, and energy. Leaders can best access this wealth of experience and empower their people by encouraging questions as a natural part of team discussions. Mike Coleman, vice president of the Alcoa Rigid Packaging business unit in Knoxville, Tennessee, told me that questions were critical in building his team:

Alcoa was in a bad position and needed a turnaround when I first joined the company. The company needed a turnaround team. By asking lots of questions with different individuals, I was able to find and develop such a team. I asked them what the problems were, what were possible solutions, how to handle internal and external problems. How to exist and move? I looked for responses like "here's my vision—what do you think?"

Questions such as the ones Sue Whitt and Mike Coleman asked can generate an atmosphere of friendly collegiality. Questions help the group recognize and reorganize its collective knowledge. As group members engage in asking questions of one another, they gradually gain a group consensus on answers and strategies since they now more clearly see each other's perspectives and also gain greater clarity of their own.

Questions, when asked at the right time in the right way, provide the glue that brings and holds the group together. Questions build strong and cohesive teams because of the many effects of questions on a group of people. Questions serve as models of responsiveness, helpfulness, and cooperation. An interesting phenomenon occurs as we ask questions about someone else's problem. The questioning process causes us become more interested in that person's problem. And when we listen to someone respond to our question, we appreciate their efforts and their attention.

Margaret Wheatley (2002) notes that leaders need to build more time for relationships and social time with teams. When leaders question, they show respect, listening, and caring. They help the group achieve group goal clarity, a most essential element toward building the team. Questions enable leaders to develop closer relationships among people. They demonstrate the questioner's ability to empathize and care about others.

Enhanced Innovation

Creativity requires asking questions for which an answer is not already known. The truth is that innovation is rarely the product of pure inspiration, that "Eureka!" moment when some genius comes up with a wholly new idea. Rather, innovation happens when people see things differently. It starts with a questioning culture that helps people gain new perspective and see things differently. Innovation is generated by great questions in an environment that encourages questions.

Pentti Sydanmaanlakka sees a questioning culture as an important foundation for innovation. "When my employees learned that I will not give answers at the beginning, but that I will first ask questions, then they learn to ask questions themselves and find solutions alone. They start questioning when they are alone." When you encourage such questions, Sydanmaanlakka says, you "create an environment which supports innovation, creativity, and a real spirit of curiosity."

Similarly, Collectcorp's Jeff Carew says that when he began to create a questioning environment in his department, new ideas blossomed:

> What resulted was something better than what was happening before I changed my leadership style. We came up with new alternatives, ones that I had not thought of. My direct reports felt a greater sense of ownership to the ideas because they belonged in part or sometimes in whole to them—and most importantly, production in my area improved. And I grew as a leader, some of the best ideas were coming from new managers because they had a fresh perspective on the environment or their situation.

Questions can also encourage people to take risks—and risks are the precursors to most of the great ideas of history. For every step forward, someone had to wonder whether a current situation could be changed or made better. Questions needed to be asked: What could happen if I did this? Is there any other way to think about this? What possibilities exist that I haven't thought of yet? For example, Columbus could have asked himself, "Is there a sea route to India?" Or Picasso, when moving to cubism, "In what other ways could I depict the human form?" (Goldberg, 1998a).

Individual Benefits of a Questioning Culture

Many of the organizational benefits just discussed also directly benefit individuals as well. For example, while the organization benefits from the results produced by motivated and empowered employees, those people benefit from the same results, of course, and also from the sense of well-being generated by that level of involvement in their work. Individuals also benefit from improved learning, greater decision-making and problem-solving abilities, and so on. Still other benefits of a questioning culture accrue primarily to individuals and only secondarily to the organizations of which they are members.

Greater Self-Awareness

Vaill (1996) points out that today's managers need a high aptitude for self-reflection and self-awareness as well as for action. Astute and clear understanding of personal motives is one of the most critical of all leadership skills. Reflective questioners, according to Vaill, become better leaders. A questioning culture encourages reflection. When we feel free to ask questions and are open to the questions of others, it heightens our need to reflect. And as we are called upon to reflect more, we become more natural at it.

Goldberg (1998a) observes that most people are totally unaware of and unconscious about the internal questions they ask themselves—even though such inquiries virtually program their thoughts, feelings, actions, and outcomes. Most of us are simply unaware of how important or pervasive our questions are to our way of thinking and acting. However, it is these very questions that serve as the basis on how we view life and make our decisions. When we are immersed in a culture that encourages questions, it helps us become more self-aware, more conscious of choices we have made, more deliberate about our decisions.

Self-reflection enables us to better understand ourselves, gaining insight into why we do some things and avoid doing other things. For example, asking the question, "Is this really worth my effort at this time?" helps you to reflect on priorities and values. How you respond can enable you to focus on what you can do to change the things you want to change. A question such as "Can you share with me why this particular issue bothers you so much?" helps you learn what is important to those around you. Questions enable you to better understand relationships in terms of how others perceive you.

People who consciously self-reflect are much more attuned to their inner feelings than those who don't, and thus likelier recognize how these feelings affect them. Reflection helps us to become more attuned to our values, more candid and authentic, and better able to speak openly about our emotions. We also become more aware of our limitations and strengths, and therefore have a more accurate self-image.

Greater Self-Confidence, Openness, and Flexibility

Organizational cultures that encourage curiosity and questions help people develop themselves. People who ask questions have more self-confidence as they see the people they question show appreciation and respect for the question and the questioner. When a non-threatening environment for questions is a daily reality, people become ever more comfortable with themselves, know their strengths better, and are more self-assured. As they see their peers and their staff demonstrate greater capability and responsibility in responding to questions and taking more initiative, leaders can be more relaxed and flexible.

In organizations that discourage questions, on the other hand, questions and those who ask them may be seen as threatening. And when questions are not responded to openly or honestly, or are actually rejected, those who ask them can feel put down and marginalized.

Questioning cultures, by generating self-confidence, also tend to encourage adaptability in meeting new challenges. People who are comfortable with questions are nimble in adjusting to fluid change and limber in their thinking in the face of new data or realities. They can juggle demands without losing focus or energy. They are comfortable with ambiguity. Questioning leaders are likely to remain calm and clear-headed under high stress or during a crisis, and remain unflappable when confronted by trying situations.

Robert Hoffman, executive director of human resources and organizational development at Novartis, highlights this aspect of a questioning culture:

> Questions have changed me immensely. I have greater self-confidence and a more relaxed attitude. I don't feel that I always have to have the answers in conversations or in situations where I need to

speak at the spur of the moment. I feel this has increased my communication skills, especially listening and persuading.

I have more trust in myself and others. Leading with questions has led to more trust, which appears to be a paradox of group life. I have stronger initiative and commitment.

I learn more as I have become more directional by more questions. I have more patience and self-control, have greater openness and transparency. I now see myself as more adaptable and flexible. I am optimistic about opportunities—more inspirational and have greater vision and cognitive capability.

Questions have given me greater understanding of organizational and political realities; I recognize the importance of organizational context and orientation. I am more willing to take risks in creating opportunities. I have a greater empathy with employees, customers, and others and a stronger commitment to develop others. My empowerment orientation is greater.

Bertrand Russell, the noted English mathematician and philosopher, once remarked that it was "a healthy thing now and then to hang a question mark on things you have long taken for granted." Leaders at all levels who question others and are able to accept questions exhibit a desire and ease in learning and improving themselves. They become more open to constructive feedback and criticism. Such leaders are more comfortable in asking people how they can better lead as well as what new leadership strengths they should cultivate.

Better Listening and Communication

When organizations develop a questioning culture, they help leaders at all levels become more empathetic and more in tune with their colleagues. People who are comfortable with asking and being asked questions have an increased ability to listen attentively and can more easily grasp the other person's perspective. Such leaders are able to get along more sensitively with people of diverse backgrounds or from other cultures. Those who lead with questions become less concerned about strict control and trust their people more. This freedom enables them to listen better and communicate in a more effective manner.

"Questions have made me sit back and be a better listener," Cargill's Douglas Eden says. "I am now much more comfortable with other people; I can more easily take an active interest in what people are saying. Questions have made my meetings more focused and effective, and have generated more solutions. I can more quickly get to the key issues."

The questions themselves force leaders to listen. Because followers see the questioning leader as more empathetic, they are willing to question and listen themselves; they hear more closely and are thus more willing to support initiatives and ideas from the leader.

Questioning leaders are adept in being persuasive and engaging when they address a group. Even when disturbing news or concerns arise, the leaders who question can retain the confidence and support of the organization. When leaders listen carefully to answers given to their questions, the people around them appreciate their efforts and attention.

Managing Conflict

Questioning leaders are better at managing conflict (Hii, 2000), because their solid questioning skills enable them to draw out all parties, understand the differing perspectives, and then find a common ideal that everyone can endorse. Hii discovered that questioning leaders are more comfortable in surfacing conflict, acknowledging the feelings and views of all sides, and then redirecting the energy toward a shared idea. They move toward a collaborative style of conflict management as opposed to being overassertive or passive and withdrawn in their approach to conflict.

Since it is generally easier to confront others and be up front with questions rather than with statements, organizations that encourage a questioning culture help people discuss issues and share concerns that otherwise might be kept hidden. Questions allow you to keep your opinions or perspectives in abeyance until you sense the interests or opinions of others.

Frank Andracchi is vice president for Constellation Generation Group. He told me how the use of questions helped him resolve serious conflict on at least two separate occasions:

> I have started to use questions in all phases of my business environment: during conversations, meetings, telephone calls, and even during the reading of documents. This process was most powerful in recent negotiations of a contract modification between Constellation and United States Steel. These negotiations were going in circles for a year before using the right questions as the vehicle to find the solution. Through the use of questions, the real issues were placed on the table and joint resolution to those issues agreed to; with both sides happy with the results.
>
> [Another set of] sites had developed a classic McCoys-versus-Hatfields attitude, causing a significant divide between the employees. This divide placed the project at risk of failure. Since the introduction of the use of questions to discuss the roots of the differences between the employees, the division has disappeared. Since this business unit discovered the use of questions, the four sites have increased to their highest level of cooperation to date.

Badaracco (2002) notes that restraint is the precondition for finding creative solutions to difficult problems. It requires that your whole mind grapple with what is really going on and what can be done. Questions enable leaders to understand and apply the essence of what Badaracco calls "quiet leadership."

Greater Understanding and Skills in Organizational and Political Realities

Questioning leaders tend to have more organizational awareness; their use of questions makes them more politically astute and better able to detect crucial networks. Questions also help leaders read and understand key power relationships. They tap into what's happening and appreciate how people feel about issues and direction in the organization. Questioning leaders know what it takes to have greater control over their organization's destiny.

In *Leading Quietly*, Badaracco comments that "creative solutions to difficult political problems rarely spring full-blown into managers' heads" (2002, p. 172). Far more often, they result from a long effort to understand, shape, and take advantage of an ever-evolving and often surprising stream of events that can be seen only through the use of questions.

Effendy Mohamed Rajab says that asking questions has helped him to become more politically sensitive: "I don't expect to get the correct answer from any single line of questioning. The correct answer is highly dependent on the context and situations from political and cultural perspectives."

Leaders improve their ability to search the unfamiliar through the use of questions. Dilworth notes how questions provide a person with leadership skills that encourage fresh thinking, and thus enable us to "avoid responding to today's problems with yesterday's solutions while tomorrow's challenges engulf us." Questions provide leaders with the opportunity to take "appropriate levels of responsibility in discovering how to develop themselves" (1998, p. 38).

Stronger Commitment to Learn and Develop

Questions not only demonstrate a greater commitment to developing others, they make you more adept at cultivating others' abilities as well as your own. Leaders who ask questions develop their emotional intelligence through questions. Questioning leaders thus improve their ability to teach, mentor, and coach.

In the process of questioning to help others learn, the leader is more likely to become a devoted learner too, someone who takes time to learn and demonstrates a love for learning and who is more clearly aware of the importance of creating great thinkers and learners throughout the organization. Through questions, people know more what leaders expect of them and are therefore more committed to learn. Through questions, colleagues know better how to set challenging but achievable goals and recognize importance of continuous learning.

Sue Whitt of Abbott Laboratories says,

> Questions have helped me learn. I loved to learn and learned a lot through questions. Questioning is a style I am comfortable with. I do not feel that I need to know everything. That's why I hired all these talented people. My joy is to deal with challenges outside my comfort zone. Questions help me to defuse tensions and to build people who enjoy working with each other.

John Morris (1991) observes that only through constant questioning do we see more clearly just who we really are, and what remarkable resources we have access to. We will also see more clearly what is really facing us, and we will become more capable of accepting and responding to change.

Stronger Leadership

Jim Collins, in his best-selling classic, *Good to Great* (2001), reports his discovery that leaders of great companies are both very humble and very persistent. In his description of "Level 5 leaders," he observes that the successful leaders of the companies he studied recognized that the title of leader does not make one a source of all wisdom. Great leaders are humbled by the realization of all they do not know. They know that asking questions of a few will not give enough data; to succeed they must make asking questions of anyone and everyone their top priority.

According to research done by Joseph Badaracco (2002), leaders who ask questions become more modest, a hallmark of Collins's Level 5 Leader. Questioning leaders are realists and don't inflate the importance of their own efforts. They take the time to drill down into problems with questions. Questioning leaders recognize that everyone is needed, and that everyone should serve one another, if the organization is to be successful.

Mark Thornhill, CEO of the Midwest Region of the American Red Cross, says, "Questions have had a significant impact on me. I now see that a true leader stands behind the follower; he is someone who is accessible to and supportive of the followers. I now lead more quietly. In reading Collins's book *Good to Great*, I learned that what great leaders do better than anyone else is question both internal and external customers."

To recap what Pentti Sydanmaanlakka told me, a questioning culture helps people "learn the skill of self-leadership." In other words, questioning helps develop leaders at all level. Through questions, as Sydanmaanlakka said, people "will also take more responsibility and be more motivated and committed."

Looking Ahead

Given the benefits of a questioning culture, how should you go about creating one? This is the topic of the next section. To pave the way, I first show how you can clear away some of the obstacles that hinder your ability to ask questions. The next chapter describes the various kinds of useful questions, and shows why not all questions are useful. I then discuss how individuals can best ask questions. And finally, I discuss how the whole organization can be imbued with a questioning culture that empowers everyone.

Part Two

ASKING QUESTIONS EFFECTIVELY

3

WHY WE HAVE TROUBLE
WITH QUESTIONS

Remember Cindy Stewart's story from Chapter One? As the "floor girl" in a sewing factory, she heard the factory managers discussing a bottleneck in the production line. "As they wrestled with solutions, none of which worked, I can clearly recall that I was thinking, 'I wish they would ask me.'" Unfortunately, many of us can see something of ourselves in those managers. They were having problems, their solutions didn't work, and they still didn't reach out to others with questions.

If, as noted in Chapter Two, the open inquiry represented by the free flow of honest questions and conversation is so powerful and beneficial, the question naturally arises: Why do we so often have trouble asking questions? In discussing this with leaders around the world, I have found that a number of answers come up consistently. We have difficulty with questions for four primary reasons:

- We avoid questions out of a natural desire to protect ourselves.
- We are too often in a rush.
- We often lack of skills in asking or answering questions due to lack of experiences and opportunities, of training, and of role models.
- We find ourselves in corporate cultures and working environments that discourage questions, especially those that challenge existing assumptions and policies.

Our Desire to Protect Ourselves

We want to protect our self-image and our image in the eyes of others; we also want to protect ourselves against uncomfortable feelings such as fear. Exposing ourselves with questions offers risks on all these fronts. But people rarely start out this way. Asking questions is a natural part of our biological makeup. Ask any parent of a child under the age of three about how children love to ask questions. Unfortunately, most of us are told by our parents, teachers, and bosses to stop asking questions. Not only are we told not to ask questions, when we do ask a question not considered appropriate or correct, we are ridiculed. From an early age, we are discouraged from asking questions, especially challenging ones, be it at home, school, or church, as questions are considered rude, inconsiderate, or intrusive. Thus we become fearful of asking any questions. As we ask fewer questions, we become ever less comfortable and competent in asking questions.

And then when we become leaders, we feel that it is important for us to have answers rather than questions. As Cindy Stewart, now president and CEO of a successful nonprofit organization, told me, "After all, we have been socialized to know the answers." Asking questions or being unable to answer questions addressed to us may show that we are unprepared to be a leader. We fear being asked questions since it may feel like an inquisition or interrogation. We have already so many times in life experienced the fear of not having the right answer and not looking good that it's easy to succumb to the temptation to avoid such situations in the future. Semler (1998) believes that managers overrate knowing where they are going, understanding what business they are in, and defining their mission. It is a macho, militaristic, and self-misleading posture. Having the courage to give up control in exchange for freedom, creativity, and inspired adaptation should be the preference of the questioning leader.

Fear inhibits us from asking questions in another way. We sometimes fear that if we ask a question we will get an answer we do not like, one that paints us as part of the problem, or one that indicates that a favored project has gone off course. When we ask questions that we truly do not know the answers to, we might get answers that cause us to change our mind or force us into an action we would prefer not to take. It is a natural human tendency to push potentially unwelcome information away. Thus we avoid asking questions especially when the answers may be threatening. Mike Coleman, vice president of Alcoa's Rigid Packaging business unit, says, "Those who have the inability to ask questions have problems with their ego."

The antidote to fear, of course, is courage. Courage is always an act, not a thought. You cannot think your way into courage; you act your way into courage. Asking questions is not always easy, especially the tough follow-up questions or questions that require deep and intensive soul-searching. A leader needs to be courageous and authentic, and not intimidated by the rank or expertise or character of the person to whom the question is posed.

Courage includes the willingness to ask questions that might challenge—even break up—current perceptions and patterns. Change also requires "challenging and altering old patterns and perceptions, for this is the very condition that allows something new to emerge" (Goldberg, 1998a, p. 9). Courage is required because to keep looking for better answers, we have to be willing to give up our current beliefs or positions. Some answers are more accurate, appropriate, and useful or moral than others. For you to want to do the hard work necessary to find better answers, you need substantial curiosity and courage. As Block (2003) once noted, it is lonely to get to the future first. It entails a large responsibility. But if leaders are not willing to do it with courageous questions, that future may not occur.

Occasionally there will be times when we must be able to challenge assumptions and beliefs in thinking and communicating—including our own. Inquiring leaders have to be able to acknowledge what they don't know and ask provocative and inspiring questions. We don't listen to someone's argument with a blank slate. We feel a sense of ownership about opinions we call our own.

It often takes incredible courage to give up on an opinion we have held for some time after listening to someone else. As critical thinkers, we have to struggle to force ourselves to try out new answers. The interplay between our old answers and new ones provides a basis for our growth.

Too often, when we encounter a question, we probably already have an answer.

Sometimes we must ask questions that we do not know the answer to. This type of behavior takes courage because asking questions and admitting we don't know an answer are behaviors not expected from leaders. We have to have willingness and courage to practice "not knowing." Leaders must be willing to "not know" or "not be right." If you are hesitant to ask questions whose answers may threaten you, consider the words of Suzanne Milchling, head of the Homeland Defense Business Unit in the Department of Defense: "It is the question *not* asked that gets me in trouble."

Not being able to risk and being fearful of asking questions traps many leaders into a cycle of inaction, defending intentions, and interpreting or explaining away others' perceptions. A well-thought-out defense or series of explanations and statements allows leaders to protect their ideal self-image. By staying focused on that image, however, leaders are prevented from seeing themselves as others do. This myopic view gets in the way of exploring others' perceptions and the leader becomes locked in a self-sealing cycle of good intentions' fueling behavior that may or may not lead to optimal results (Bianco-Mathis, Nabors, and Roman, 2002).

Fear generally makes the leader focus on the followers, and to be sure that if results are not achieved, it is the followers' problem. Rarely does the leader's risk-averse focus leave room to turn inward and explore "what can I do differently" or "how am I contributing to this situation." The lack of information keeps such leaders in the dark and creates confusion for everyone else, who may in turn decide to work around them or withdraw to pursue their own objectives outside the leaders' reach. A leader who is willing to take risks will ask the questions that need to be asked.

We Are Too Often in a Rush

People become leaders in organizations for many reasons, but one of the primary reasons is that they build track records as problem solvers and being able to get results. This builds a pattern of behavior in which we are too focused on fixing problems right away so that we can check them off our to-do list and move on. Chad Holliday, chairman and CEO of DuPont, points to this sort of impatience as a reason some executives have trouble with questions. "It requires self-discipline to keep questioning," he says. "There is a great temptation to make statements, especially when you are in a hurry and want to do things quickly. This morning, I discovered that something should have been done two weeks ago. My first reaction was to tell them to 'get it done.'" But, he adds, he managed to resist this impulse and ask what happened and why. "I get better results this way," he says. Too often, leaders lack the self-discipline Holliday displayed.

When we use questions, we should not just be sharing information but sharing responsibility. Rather than telling people what to do, the leader must have the courage to ask them what needs to be done and then make a serious attempt to remove any obstacles in the way. This not only generates the best ideas but also gives people a stake in the success of an effort. If you want people to be there for the crash landing, you'd better invite them to the launch.

Few practical ideas are more obvious and critical than the need to get perspective in the midst of action. We all get swept up into the action, particularly when it becomes intense or personal. Self-reflection does not come naturally. Charles Ostland, principal of Oakton High School, says, "I found that in terms of leadership, I must personally work hard to become more reflective and ask more questions of people in an attempt to help them clarify their own opinion and position on an issue, rather than providing my own opinion or answer." Like many leaders, he says he has a "natural tendency to jump to a quick answer or give an initial opinion about something" before asking others for their views and solutions.

Asking the right question is not an easy task, especially when the group is struggling with an overwhelming problem or fighting alligators. As Revans (1982) notes, "the capacity to ask fresh questions in conditions of ignorance, risk, and confusion, when nobody knows what to do next" is at the heart of great leadership.

Leaders must maintain the capacity for reflection, even in the fog of war. This capability is similar to the ability of great athletes who can at once play the game and observe it as a whole, what may be referred to as contemplation in action. Heifetz and Linsky (2002) note that a big-picture leader needs to "get on the balcony," to notice the various patterns that are occurring. Being temporarily above the hustle and bustle of the crowd is important, to take the mental activity of stepping back in the midst of action and asking, What's really going on here?

Having the ability to do critical thinking and ask critical questions that can lead to clarity, precision, and accuracy is the sign of a leader who is concerned with truly making a difference and not just going for a quick fix. "In the final analysis, I learned that there is no such thing as the correct answers, it is only perspective," Effendy Mohamed Rajab told me. Rajab, the senior training and development director for the World Organization of the Scout Movement in Geneva, Switzerland, said that questions should be "designed to understand any issue from the perspectives of the respondents, but not necessarily the correct answers. Simply put, if you don't ask, you don't know for sure why things happen the way they happen."

Lack of Skills in Asking Questions

Many of us don't know how to ask questions for the simple reason that we are out of practice (not having practiced since our parents told us to stop asking so many questions at the age of three). We may have received thousands of hours of teaching in classrooms and training in the workplace on history, mathematics, computers, diversity, and leadership, but never anything on the asking of questions. The asking of questions, especially how to ask great questions, has never appeared in any of our curricula or on any of our performance appraisals. We have never gotten feedback on the quality of our questions. And rarely have we had a boss who was a model of an inquiring leader, someone who could demonstrate the skill, power, and benefit of questions.

Mark Harper, president of wholesale marketing for ConocoPhillips Petroleum, says that it took a while for him to gain skill in using questions as a management tool: "At the beginning it was uncomfortable and frustrating. I didn't know how to ask good questions. I had a tendency to ask too many leading questions, or I only asked questions when I knew I had to make a decision."

As Harper's comment demonstrates, even when we do ask questions, we find the process uncomfortable and frustrating. Too often, when we ask questions, we provoke defensiveness. We ask what we think is a simple question, such as "Why did that happen?" and people react as if we were accusing them of dereliction of duty. Or we ask an innocent question about a decision the boss has made and the boss reacts angrily, as if to a direct challenge. In other words, even when we do ask questions, we do not do so skillfully, in a way that elicits a frank but friendly response. When we lack questioning skills, all too often our questions are limited, incorrect, or simplistic. Ineffective questions lead to detours, missed goals, and costly mistakes. Goldberg (1998a) notes that, depending on how the leader asks a question, it can be perceived as "an invitation, a request, or a missile." Because questions are so powerful and can be provocative and challenging, we must be skilled in their use (Nadler & Chandon, 2004).

Asking good questions requires two critical skills. First, you must know *what* questions to ask, for questions are not all created equal. Second, you must know *how* to ask them. Chapters Four and Five offer guidelines on how to ask the right questions effectively.

Corporate Cultures Can Discourage Questions

Our environment or culture determines a large part of our personal behavior. For example, I behave very differently in a church than I do at a football game—same person but totally different behavior in different contexts. Likewise, I behave differently as a father than I do when I am with former college roommates—same person but in very different roles. Thus some of us may feel much more comfortable asking our child a question than we ever could asking our boss a question.

In some corporate cultures and with some bosses, it would be taboo and dangerous to ask too many questions, especially questions that might rock the boat or cause someone to lose face.

Thus we become afraid to question authority. In addition to corporate cultures and expected roles for those cultures, Americans live in a national culture that, as Yankelovich (1999) and many cultural anthropologists have noted, "rushes to action." In the face of any problem, we Americans tend to say, "What are we going to *do* about it?" We perceive thinking and reflecting as unproductive use of time (even though we admire a person such as Einstein who would frequently be found in his office at Princeton staring into space).

And many corporate cultures have an aversion to listening to any news that isn't good. As Sidney Finkelstein writes in *Why Smart Executives Fail*, "It's especially easy for executives to accept good news unquestioningly and to investigate further only when there seems to be a problem" (2003, p. 200). "Enron, WorldCom, and a long list of dot-coms all had corporate boards that refrained from questioning their policies or even looking too closely at what they were doing, because their stock prices were soaring." When the board refuses to ask questions, that sends a powerful signal throughout the organization for people to keep their heads down.

Oftentimes, new ideas are not allowed to occur in an organization as they might conflict with existing, established mental models or ways of doing things. Questioning leaders have the task of confronting these assumptions without evoking defensiveness or anger. They must be able to surface and test the mental models and basic assumptions of colleagues. Asking questions that are challenging requires risk, occasional conflict, and instability because addressing the issues underlying problems may involve upending deep and entrenched norms. Questioning leaders are confident and willing to challenge beliefs and assumptions.

Leaders must continuously look for "white-space opportunities"—that is, new areas of growth possibilities that fall between the cracks because they don't naturally match the skills of existing business units. They look for "strategic intent," that is, a tangible corporate goal or destiny that represents a stretch for the organization. For example, at Wal-Mart everyone is encouraged to look for things that don't seem right and ask questions. It is called "ETDT: eliminate the dumb things."

Heifetz and Linsky (2002) note that people expect leaders to provide them with right answers, not to confront them with disturbing questions and difficult choices. That's why the initial challenge and risk of exercising leadership is to go beyond your authority—to put your credibility and position on the line in order to tackle the problems at hand. Without the willingness to challenge people's expectations of you, there is no way you can escape being dominated by the social system and its inherent limits.

Chapter Six explains how you can build a questioning culture in your team and organization.

Confronting Our Discomfort with Questions

This combination of fear, time pressure, lack of skills, and discouraging corporate culture all result in many leaders asking relatively few questions, and asking questions oftentimes only out of a sense of desperation. But, as the leaders I interviewed for this book show, it doesn't have to be that way.

Take Frank Andracchi, vice president of Constellation Generation Group, an energy company. He told me:

> I have started to use questions in all phases of my business environment: during conversations, meetings, telephone calls, and even

during the reading of documents. Personally, I have found that since using questions—or more correctly stated—as I listen to any conversation and think of questions to obtain more information, I learn more, know more, and improve my comprehension. Additionally, as an executive, I find I interfere significantly less during any meeting or conversation. The "brain switch" to thinking of questions has been extremely powerful, taking my leadership up another step.

And Jeff Carew, vice president of collections for Collectcorp, has also made the transition from telling to asking:

> I discovered that I was leading by telling rather than teaching—or by giving answers not asking questions—after a 360-degree leadership evaluation program. . . . This feedback initiated a change in the way I managed my staff. Now I refuse to give the answer to problems; I ask questions of them on how to make things better in their area, or how to approach something differently. At first they were skeptical but eventually got with the program.
>
> Collectcorp is becoming more of a classroom, where I am a facilitator for my group rather than the guy in the corner who will give you the answer to everything.
>
> I am making a bigger impact in my team's growth. And their confidence is growing because they know the answer to their problems is in their heads. My job is to help them get it out.

Many executives told me that the simple act of asking questions has brought about profound change. For example, Robert Hoffman, executive director for organization development at Novartis, whom I quoted in Chapter Two, is worth repeating here:

> Questions have given me greater understanding of organizational and political realities; I recognize the importance of organizational context and orientation. I am more willing to take risks in creating opportunities. I have a greater empathy with employees, customers, and others and a stronger commitment to develop others. My empowerment orientation is greater.

Another leader who experienced personal growth from adopting a questioning leadership style is Tom Laughlin, president of Caravela, an international leadership and team development consulting firm:

> Questions have made an absolute difference to me as a leader. I don't have to have all the answers anymore. It has caused me to think differently. I have gone from trying to find solutions to often superficial symptoms to now getting to the real problem. I am actually a better problem solver because I am a better problem identifier.
>
> Questions have made me a better coach and mentor. Questions allow me to check out my sense of where I am and should be. They allow me to express my emotion and intuition and understanding. People think more highly of me. People feel more encouraged.

When we learn to use questions, not only do we experience personal growth, we help our whole team. Says Suzanne Milchling, "I use questions so as to get buy-in so that all are on the same page. Questions allow us to have a common understanding and to make us think of all the steps in the process. . . . By asking questions of yourself and others, you are able to round out the understanding of the situation for all."

Morris remarks that only "through constant questioning do we see more clearly just who we really are, and what remarkable resources we have access to. We will also see more clearly what is really facing us, and we will become more capable of accepting and responding to change" (1991, p. 79). Cindy Stewart's experience as a leader certainly supports this:

> When I became CEO of the Family Health Council of Central Pennsylvania, Inc. in 1999, I needed to shift the culture from a task-oriented hierarchy to a functional, empowered team environment. By leading through questions, I was able to act as a role model and demonstrate my willingness to learn, my desire to serve, and that humility can be inspiring. My employees have come to understand that I am a consultative leader and that it is critical to our success

that they are knowledgeable of their customer expectations, willingly bring key information to the work process, and seek opportunity for continuous quality improvement. In the past four years, we have increased our budget by $3.5 million, have opened a new direct service site, and received funding for five new programs. This could not have happened without empowering the staff and unleashing their creativity through questions.

Perhaps Chad Holliday, chairman and CEO of DuPont, sums it all up best: "On critical issues, I believe that we must use questions."

This chapter has uncovered the factors that may cause us to have trouble with questions, showing that those factors can be overcome. The testimony from the many leaders supports this point: It can be done. Questions can become an effective management and leadership tool for us when we are comfortable with asking questions, we know what kinds of questions to ask, and we are effective at eliciting full responses to questions and listening to those responses effectively. Those are the topics of the next chapters.

4

ASKING THE RIGHT QUESTIONS

It is important for leaders to fully recognize and understand the power of words. The words we choose to use are metaphors for concepts that define our attitudes and behaviors, structures and concepts. Kouzes and Posner note that "our words evoke images of what we hope to create and how we expect people to behave" (2002, p. 91). The questions that a leader asks send messages about the focus of the organization. They are indeed indicators of what's of most concern to the leader. Our questions are an important measure of how serious we are about our espoused beliefs.

A key for leaders in asking questions is contextual: What do I want my question to accomplish? The questions we employ provide feedback about which values should be attended to and how much energy should be devoted to them. Thus we should be reflecting on what questions we should be asking if we want people to focus on integrity, or on trust. Other questions would demonstrate our concern with customer or client satisfaction, or quality, innovation, growth, or personal responsibility.

Questions can be very powerful in focusing attention. When leaders ask questions, they send constituents on mental journeys— quests—in search of answers. These journeys can be positive and productive, inspiring creative problem solving, new insights, and fresh perspective. Unfortunately, our questions can also send people on journeys that are negative and unproductive, provoking defensiveness and self-doubt.

Questions That Empower and Disempower

As Chapter Three notes, one of the reasons that questions cause trouble is that we often ask the wrong questions, that is, questions that disempower others. Questions that disempower focus on the reasons why the person did not or cannot succeed. Such questions result in a defensive or reactive mode, immediately casting the blame on the other person. (Sometimes leaders do this to escape any blame or responsibility themselves.) Poor questions drain energy from the individual and cause reaction rather than creation. Here are some examples of such questions:

- Why are you behind schedule?
- What's the problem with this project?
- Who isn't keeping up?
- Don't you know better than that?

We end up creating that what we focus on. By asking disempowering questions, the leader closes the gateway to identifying paths to success. Such questions prevent people from having the opportunity to clarify misunderstandings or achieve goals. *What's wrong* questions threaten self-esteem and thereby cause people to get mired in their problems. And, once in this defensive mode, people are more likely to see themselves as part of the problem rather than as the source of possible solutions.

Empowering questions, on the other hand, get people to think and allow them to discover their own answers, thus developing self-responsibility and transference of ownership for the results. Such questions can help them realize how they are contributing to the whole. Empowering questions build positive attitudes and self-esteem; they remove blocks and open people up to unexpected possibilities while inviting discovery, creativity, and innovation.

Empowering questions help develop alignment within teams and draw out the optimum performance from individual members and the team as a whole. They create a high-energy, high-trust environment and enable people to identify, clarify, and express their wants or needs. Such questions encourage people to take risks, nurture deep relationships, and dissolve resistance to change. Empowering questions enhance your energy level as they focus on what is already working, what can become energizing and supportive, and how best to clarify and achieve common objectives. They also focus on benefits and yield responses that support movement forward toward the objectives.

Jean Halloran, HR manager for Hewlett-Packard, notes that in empowering others, the leader has to resist the urge to give people advice. When people ask for help, the leader needs to ask questions so that they come up with their own answers.

So instead of asking the disempowering questions such as "Why are you behind schedule?" or "What's the problem with this project?" Marilee Goldberg (1998a) suggests that leaders ask questions such as these:

- How do you feel about the project thus far?
- What have you accomplished so far that you are most pleased with?
- How would you describe the way you want this project to turn out?
- Which of these objectives do you think will be easiest to accomplish? Which will be most difficult?
- What will be the benefits for our customers if you can meet all these objectives—for our company, for our team, for you personally?
- What key things need to happen to achieve the objective? What kind of support do you need to assure success?

Roots of Great Questions

Superb questions accomplish a number of wonderful results. So what constitutes a great question for the leader to ask? There is no single correct answer, of course, but most of us who have experience with great questions would agree that they can create the following benefits:

- Cause the person to focus and to stretch.
- Create deep reflection.
- Challenge taken-for-granted assumptions that prevent people from acting in new and forceful ways.
- Generate courage and strength.
- Lead to breakthrough thinking.
- Contain the keys that open the door to great solutions.
- Enable people to better view the situation.
- Open doors in the mind and get people to think more deeply.
- Test assumptions and cause individuals to explore why they act in the way that they do as well as why they choose to take action.
- Generate positive and powerful action.

Revans (1982) noted that great questions are fresh questions raised in "conditions of ignorance, risk, confusion, or when nobody knows what to do next." Great questions are selfless, not asked to illustrate the cleverness of the questioner or to generate information or an interesting response for the questioner. They are generally supportive, insightful, and challenging. They are often unpresumptuous and offered in a sharing spirit.

Great questions are asked at the time when it generates the strongest amount of reflection and learning. Inquisitive leaders make good use of informal meetings, with no script, agenda, or set of action items to discuss. Instead they start out with empowering questions such as "What's on your mind? Can you tell me about that? Can you help me understand? What should we be worried about?"

Mark Harper, president of wholesale marketing for ConocoPhillips Petroleum, shared some of his favorite questions with me.

Several effective questions work well for me, including the following:

- What is a viable alternative?
- What are the advantages and disadvantages you see in this suggestion?
- Can you more fully describe your concerns?
- What are your goals?
- How would you describe the current reality?
- What are a few options for improvement?
- What will you commit to do by when?

The better the question, the greater the insight gained and the better the solution attained. Tailor your question to the individual you are talking to. Suzanne Milchling, head of the Homeland Defense Business Unit in the Department of Defense, explains how she chooses the questions she asks:

> The most valuable questions for me are those that turn individuals to look inward at how they are perceived by others. When I ask some of the employees, "How are you going to do the project?" I get a straight answer. Those I call direct; I can direct them to do something and they answer my questions in a direct and linear manner.
>
> For other, more abstract thinkers, I need them to cycle within. So I like asking questions like "Would it be useful to get Jim's ideas first? Would he be able to grease the skids for you?" Getting such individuals to recycle their thought patterns in slow motion and out loud to me and others raises questions within them that they may not have thought of before. The abstract thinkers, like my son Robert, need to be made aware of the details. Their thinking is in patterns and I want them to understand the "detail" thinkers—the people they may have to convince—the people who think in details and linearly.

Oftentimes, the best, easiest and most effective way to ask a good question is to simply build on a previous question or on the response to that question. The art and science of careful listening and then generating an open-ended, creative question will quickly and constructively move individuals toward great insights and effective actions.

Types of Effective Questions

Effective questions are those that accomplish their purpose as well as build a positive relationship between the questioner and questionee. Of course, leaders can ask a variety of types of questions, depending on whether the purpose is to build the individual's or group's capacity to understand and reframe the problem, to build common goals, to develop potential strategies, or to take effective action. Questions should not only build a deeper and better understanding of the problem and possible solutions but should also construct better working relations among the problem solvers. Broadly speaking, questions come in two types: open-ended questions and closed questions. Closed questions seek a short, specific response, like yes or no. By contrast, open-ended questions give the person or group a high degree of freedom in deciding how to respond. Consider the following examples. The topic is the same in both questions, but the responses you get will probably be very different.

- How have sales been going?
- Did you make your sales goal?

Open-Ended Questions

Open-ended questions encourage people to expand ideas and allow exploration of what's important to them or what is comfortable for them to reveal; they also encourage people to do the work of self-reflection and problem solving rather than justifying or defending a position. "I find the open-ended questions most powerful in getting people to respond openly without restricting them to a focus," Effendy Mohamed Rajab told me.

Asking open-ended, unbiased questions also shows respect for the views of others. Open-ended questions invite others to "tell their story" in their own words. They help to establish rapport, gather information, and increase understanding. When asked properly, they do not lead people toward a specific answer. When asking open-ended questions one must be ready and willing to listen to the response, which may take a while to unfold, and which may prompt further questions for clarification.

Open-ended questions should begin with words such as "why" and "how" or phrases such as "What do you think about . . . ." Open-ended questions can help people think analytically and critically. Ultimately, a good open-ended question should stir discussion and debate. Useful phrases to use with open-ended questions include:

What do you think about . . . ?

Could you say more about . . . ?

What possibilities come to mind? What might happen if you . . . ?

What do you think you will lose if you give up [the point under discussion]?

What have you tried before?

What do you want to do next?

Depending on the scope of the question, you may need to coach others through the question by breaking it down into more specific parts. For example, "What do you think of our strategic plan?" is such a broad question that people may grope for a way to begin answering it. You can break it down by homing in on a specific aspect of the strategic plan, such as "What would you identify as the major threats and opportunities we face?"

Why Questions. *Why* questions are perhaps the most important types of open-ended questions for leaders to ask as these questions force everyone to go into deeper layers of cause and effect, and of purposes and assumptions. Such questions are necessary to get under the surface to places where you need to go in order to solve the problem. Although *why* questions may be difficult or uncomfortable for both the leader and the person questioned, they are essential for understanding the deep causes of the situation and they generate deep learning for the questionee.

Jeff Carew, vice president of collections at Collectcorp, offers this view of the importance of *why* questions:

> What comes out of these discussions is almost always new alternatives that none of us had entered the meeting with. When the staff recognize that I am not going to give "the answer," it is incumbent on them to think. Questions that are most effective are most often ones where there is no clear right or wrong answer, ones that allow us to engage in conversation.
>
> An example may be: "I have noticed that volumes have increased dramatically in your area over the last few days, what do you attribute it to?" I will ask the same question again and if they have only part of the answer, I send them off again until I am satisfied that they have probed all possible reasons. Then we will get together as a group and come up with solutions to the "volume issue."

Remember that *why* questions are really quite natural—we all asked them all the time when we were children. However, they became uncomfortable as we grew up because they caused our or someone else's authority or expertise to be doubted. When asking *why* questions, the leader should watch the tone of voice. The *why* question should indicate curiosity and a search for knowledge, and not anger or frustration.

Why questions are valuable and frequently become great questions as they cause us to reflect and to perhaps see things in fresh, unpredictable ways. Questions such as "Why do you think that?" or "Why did this work?" can help the group examine old issues in new, original ways. Here are some other examples of questions that could produce rich responses:

- Can that be done in any other way?
- What other options can we think of?
- What resources have we never used?
- What do we expect to happen if we do that?
- What would happen if you did nothing at all?
- What other options do you have?
- What is stopping us?
- What happens if . . . ?
- Have we ever thought of . . . ?

At Toyota, employees are taught to think *why* consecutively five times. This is an adaptation of cause-and-effect thinking. If employees think *why* and find a cause, they try to ask themselves *why* again. They continue five times. Through these five *whys*, they can break down causes into a very specific level. This five-times-why approach is very useful for solving problems.

DuPont Chairman Chad Holliday echoes Toyota's approach. "I believe that one has to ask the *why* question three times to get to the core why," he told me. "*Why* questions have the most power. Most of the time people answer with a surface response to the first why question. For example, safety is very important to us and we believe that most if not all injuries can be prevented. Someone's finger was cut in a machine. Why?—Because the employee put his finger in machine. Why?—Because the machine was not functioning. Why?—Because maintenance had not been scheduled."

Other Types of Open-Ended Questions. Other types of open-ended questions have a wide variety of uses. Specific types of open-ended questions include the following:

- *Explorative questions* open up new avenues and insights and lead to new explorations: Have you explored or thought of . . . ? Would such a source help . . . ?

- *Affective questions* invite members to share feelings about an issue: How do you feel about leaving this job?

- *Reflective questions* encourage more exploration and elaboration: You said there are difficulties with your manager; what do think causes these difficulties?

- *Probing questions* invite the person or group to go more deeply into a particular issue, to examine thoroughly or to question closely. This is useful not only for getting more information, but for getting people to be more open and expansive in their thinking; words such as *describe*, *explain*, *clarify*, *elaborate*, or *expand* get into more depth or breadth on a topic. For example: Can you elaborate on why this is happening?

- *Fresh questions* challenge basic assumptions: Why must it be that way? What do you always . . .? Has this ever been tried?

- *Questions that create connections* establish a systems perspective: What are the consequences of these actions?

- *Analytical questions* examine causes and not just symptoms: Why has this happened?

- *Clarifying questions* help free us from ambiguity, but such questions are sometimes difficult to ask. When we hear a question, we tend to think we should know what the other person means, and that it is some fault of ours that we are not able to understand. Possible questions to ask: What specifically did you mean by that? How exactly would you like that done? Could you explain more about this situation?

People often think of probing questions as a form of attack, but it doesn't need to be that way. "I ask probing questions because my people want to look good and I want them to look good." Suzanne Milchling told me. "The goal is to get them to learn on their own." When I asked how probing questions help people to look good, she replied, "It is the question that was unanticipated and not asked that gets our people in trouble."

Working with Open-Ended Questions. Open-ended questions can address either content or process issues, and content and process questions have different roles. Spitzer and Evans (1997) distinguish them as follows: content questions ask about the data used to solve a problem or make a decision, and process questions focus on how the problem was solved or the decision made. Both are essential to good problem solving and decision making.

Most leaders focus on content questions, which come more naturally; process questions, on the other hand, require conscious attention. Starting with the appropriate process questions gives people access to insights that help them formulate and explain their thinking. In comparison, starting with content questions risks leading people and limiting the range of their responses. Thus, the preferred sequence is to start with process questions and then proceed to content questions.

Some leaders are uncomfortable asking open-ended questions, since by definition, they allow the respondent to take the conversation to new places. In other words, open-ended questions give a large measure of control to the person who answers. Leaders who like to maintain control tend to focus on closed questions, which only call for a brief response and allow the questioner to decide what to say or ask next. Asking closed questions can become a habit. But as we learn to ask open-ended questions, the people in the organization benefit as they think through their responses to express what they want to say. And with their answers, we find out more about what they think and feel from *their* perspective.

Ask lots of open-ended questions. Open-ended questions that begin with *Why?* or *How?* get people thinking and talking. You may be surprised at how much talk you unleash. You may learn a lot, and even if you just listen, they'll walk away happy and feeling heard and respected.

Closed Questions

Closed questions call for a specific answer, either yes or no, or call for the respondent to select an answer from a limited range of choices. Closed questions often begin with *what, when,* or *how many,* or ask the respondent to agree or disagree with a statement. Here are some examples of closed questions:

- How many people will be affected?
- Did you agree with this decision?
- When should we meet?
- What time is it?
- Do you prefer Plan A or Plan B?

As noted, open-ended questions tend to explore possibilities, feelings, and reasons why. In contrast, closed questions tend to focus on facts: what, when, where. Because they call for specific responses, closed questions also tend to be quick and easy to answer.

Closed questions are useful at the beginning and end of conversations. As you start a conversation, asking a simple closed question it makes it easy for people to answer and doesn't force them to reveal too much about themselves. For example, you might begin a conversation by asking, "Is this a good time for us to talk?" At the end of a conversation, closed questions can help you clarify or seek further understanding of the results of the discussion and reach closure on a decision or course of action. Salespeople often use closed questions when they move in to close the sale: "If I can deliver this tomorrow, will you sign for it now?"

If you are not clear about what another person is saying, a direct closed question can quickly clarify the situation. Open-ended questions, as discussed earlier, can also be used for clarification, but closed questions are often more direct: "It sounds like you're saying that we need to speed up action on this. Is that right?" or "Do you want me to take you off the project?" Such questions help bring exploratory discussions launched by open-ended questions down to earth, remove vagueness and ambiguity, and help move the group forward.

Of course, all these questions can be followed up with additional questions. Follow-up questions are usually even more powerful since they enable you to acquire a deeper understanding of the situation, demonstrate that you were listening, and enable you to achieve double- and triple-loop levels of learning.

Unhelpful Questions

Besides disempowering questions, two other types of questions that are not helpful from the leader are *leading questions*, those that force or encourage the person or group to respond in the way intended by the questioner (You wanted to do it by yourself, didn't you?) or *multiple questions*, a string of questions put together to meet the needs of the questioner but confusing to the responder.

Leading questions either include the answer within the question (Don't you agree that John is the problem here?), come with extra baggage that suggests the expected answer (What do you think about John? I don't think he's a team player. . .), or include some form of carrot or stick to prod the other person to produce the expected answer (Everyone else on the team thinks John is the problem. What about you?).

The problem with leading questions is that they are not genuine attempts to seek information; they are not-so-subtle efforts to influence, persuade, or coerce agreement. They are not questions at all. When there is a power discrepancy between the questioner and the respondent, the effect of leading questions can be alienation and disempowerment. Even when no power imbalance is involved, leading questions can fray relationships.

Multiple questions, especially if they are closed questions, can result in the person being subjected to them feeling interrogated. It is tempting—and often accurate—for the respondent to feel that the questioner has a private agenda that does not concern itself with anyone else's well-being or opinions.

Finding Great Questions

Recognize that the search for great questions is never completed. Peter Senge et al. (1999) offers these suggestions as to where to search for great questions:

- *Assessing the landscape:* Get a feel for the larger context; scan the horizon as well as the contours of the current business landscape; notice indicators that point to storms as well as sunny skies.
- *Discovering core questions:* Look for patterns for questions, cluster the questions, and consider the relationships that appear among them; notice what pops up in order to uncover the deeper themes that the initial questions reveal.
- *Creating images of possibilities:* Imagine what the situation would be if big questions were answered; create vivid images of possibilities.
- *Evolving workable strategies:* Workable strategies begin to emerge in response to compelling questions and to the images of possibility that these questions evoke.

Throughout the pages of this book, you will see numerous examples of types of great questions for various purposes. In the next chapter, I turn to ways to ask these questions.

5

THE ART OF ASKING QUESTIONS

Grasping the art of questioning can lead to impressive results; asking inappropriate questions usually closes off learning. But even when we work hard to make sure the questions we ask are appropriate, we can undermine the process by asking questions carelessly. The attitude, mindset, pace, timing, environment, and context can all affect the impact of our questions. A question asked at the right time in the right manner with the right person is just as important as the content of the question itself. Good questions can become great questions when the science of inquiring is blended with the art of questioning.

Judging Versus Learning: The Mindset for Asking Questions

As Adams (2004) emphasizes, our mindset frames how we see the world. It simultaneously programs what we believe to be our personal limitations and what we see as our possibilities. Mindsets define the parameters of our actions and interactions and affect, either explicitly or implicitly, outcomes in any area of focus. They are a determinant in the types of questions we ask ourselves and others. In addition, our individual mindset determines how we observe, understand, and accept ourselves and others.

Adams refers to two types of mindsets that may reside in the questioner: learner and judger. In the *learner* mindset, the questioner seeks to be responsive to life's circumstances. When we are focused on learning, we seek to understand the past as a way of guiding our actions in the future. Leaders with the learning mindset tend to be optimistic and presuppose new possibilities, a hopeful future, and sufficient resources. They exude optimism, possibilities, and hope.

The *judger* mindset, on the other hand, is reactive. Leaders with the judging mindset tend to focus on the past, not as a means of learning but to apportion praise or, more likely, blame. When our focus is on judging, we worry more about fixing responsibility for problems than on working with others to find solutions. Judging questions result in win-lose encounters as they all too often operate in an attack-or-defend paradigm. Leaders with the judging mentality tend to believe they know the answers already anyway.

Leaders who focus on learning rather than judging can be flexible and relate to others in a win-win manner that facilitates the search for creative solutions. Such leaders employ relationships that operate in a collaborative and innovative mode. A leader with the learner mindset can be more open to new possibilities than one who prefers to judge, and less attached to personal opinions and the need to be right.

"It is important to be benign when asking questions," says Michael Coleman, president of Alcoa's Rigid Packaging business unit in Knoxville, Tennessee. "Seek the cause without being accusatory. I firmly believe that the strength of questions is a tried-and-true way to find root causes. I take care in how I ask questions. I do not demonstrate with my body language that my mind is made up, that a person is being attacked or getting sabotaged. If I act in this way, I do not get the full or complete answer; the person worries more about getting into trouble and being foolish than about listening to and responding to my questions."

According to Adams, the learning mindset exemplified by Michael Coleman leads to much greater effectiveness, breakthroughs, and transformations. Although it may sometimes be more difficult and challenging to operate with a learner mindset, it is much more rewarding for everyone involved. Learning mindsets lead to thinking objectively, creating solutions, and relating in a win-win way. Leaders with learner mindsets ask genuine questions, that is, questions to which they don't already know the answers. Consider another comment by Michael Coleman: "I believe that leaders often misuse questions. I use questions to gain knowledge or to teach. I don't ask questions that I already know the answers to or to embarrass someone—this sabotages the whole purpose of questions."

A leader who is habitually judgmental, on the other hand, puts employees on the defensive because they live in constant fear of being judged and found wanting. A judging attitude causes employees to hide their mistakes, defend their behavior, and refuse to ask for help or admit their weaknesses or vulnerabilities. This can lead to a vicious spiral.

Exhibit 5.1 summarizes these two divergent mindsets as well as divergent relationships, which in turn result in totally different questions and questioning styles on the part of the leader.

Here are some examples of questions asked from the learning mindset, according to Adams:

- What's good or useful about this?
- What possibilities does this open up?
- What can we do about this?
- How can we stay on track?
- What can we learn from this?

For contrast, here are some examples of judging questions:

- Why is this a failure?
- What's wrong with you?
- Whose fault is it?
- Why can't you get it right?

By consciously adopting a learning mindset, we can become more open to new possibilities and ask questions more effectively.

Exhibit 5.1 Learner-Judger Mindset
and Relationships Chart

Mindsets

Judger	Learner
Judgmental (of self and others)	Accepting (of self and others)
Reactive and automatic	Responsive and thoughtful
Know-it-already	Values not knowing
Blame	Responsibility
Inflexible and rigid	Flexible and adaptive
Either/or thinking	Both/and thinking
Self-righteous	Inquisitive
Personal perspective only	Considers perspectives of others
Defends assumptions	Questions assumptions
More statements and opinions	More questions and curiosity
Possibilities seen as limited	Possibilities seen as unlimited
Primary mood: protective	Primary mood: curiosity

We all have both mindsets, and we have the power to choose where we operate from in any moment.

Relationships

Judger	Learner
Win-lose relationships	Win-win relationships
Sense of being separate	Sense of being connected
Fears differences	Values differences
Debates	Dialogues
Criticizes	Critiques
Listens for:	Listens for:
• Right/wrong	• Facts
• Agree/disagree	• Understanding
• Differences	• Commonalities
Feedback perceived as rejection	Feedback perceived as worthwhile
Seeks to attack or defend	Seeks to resolve and create

We all relate from both mindsets, and we have the power to choose how we relate in any moment.

Source: Adapted from Marilee G. Adams, *Change Your Questions, Change Your Life*, San Francisco: Berrett-Koehler, 2004.

When those around us sense that we do have a learning attitude, that we are eager for new information and new insights, they will be more open and thoughtful in answering our questions. The flow of information and ideas will open up, and problem solving, teamwork, and innovation will be enhanced.

Adopting a Learning Attitude

It can be difficult in a high-pressure business environment to get away from a judging mindset. After all, managers are responsible for results; they must make sure that people are held accountable. When the results don't measure up, when things go wrong, the manager has to find out what happened and why. But notice, finding out *what* happened and *why* does not mean finding out *who*. Indeed, effective leaders know that the question of who must often be left off the table to get accurate answers to the questions of what and why. Even when issues of who must be addressed, effective leaders know that the best approach is to be the supportive coach rather than the judging boss.

Coaching is the opposite of bossing. A coaching-type relationship helps people work out issues and find their own answers through the skillful use of probing questions. A supportive attitude of mutual discovery on the part of the leader creates trust and builds support in return. Coaches help employees recognize their strengths and uncover their blind spots; they can offer additional possibilities and options that employees had not considered in evaluating their situations. Such leaders listen carefully and thoroughly, especially when they don't like or agree with what they are hearing, and they are willing to suspend their own opinions in the face of new data.

Such leaders possess a set of attitudes and dispositions that encourage them to want to ask useful questions and to ask them in a fair-minded way. They are not concerned with who is right; whoever finds the better conclusion first is not relevant; what matters is the search for better conclusions. If you give signals to those around you that you are their partner in a discovery process intended to enrich you both, they will see your critical questions as a tool that is indispensable to both of you.

Sue Whitt, global head of Abbott Labs' Pharmaceutical Regulatory Operations, explained to me how she used questions to help take the edge off being the boss and develop a coaching relationship with her staff: "Through the use of questions, I could mitigate some of the negative that comes with positional power," she told me. "I got a lot of energy from my staff as questions helped them forget that I had this authority. Questions actually led to a dialogue. When projects were off track, I asked them to think of times why they made that choice. This got them thinking and speaking. I would ask, 'Why did you take this path? How does this connect to the goals set?' By asking why and what questions (simple but effective), less often than who and when questions, I was much more effective at [helping them navigate] the system. I could give them some of the who and when; but not the what and the why."

Here are some specific suggestions that can help you coach others and adopt a learning attitude:

- Respond without judging the thoughts, feelings, or situations of other people.
- Consider yourself a beginner, regardless of experience.
- Avoid focusing on your own role (which can lead to a self-protective approach) and take the role of an outside observer, researcher, or reporter.
- Look at the situation from multiple perspectives, especially your respondents'.
- Look for win-win solutions.
- Be tolerant of yourself and of others.
- Ask clarifying questions.
- Accept change as constant and embrace it.

How to Frame Questions

Framing questions involves much more than choosing the right words to express them. Questions are framed by the entire context that surrounds them. Indeed the most important part of framing questions has already been discussed: asking questions as a part of a learning process rather than a judging exercise. By making clear that our questions are attempts to learn, we have already gone a long way toward framing them in a way that will yield positive results. Conversely, if our attitude is critical and judgmental, no preamble and no amount of wordsmithing will overcome the larger message our attitude sends. David Smyk of Healthcare Executive Partners says, "The proper framing of questions allows one to view the questioner as a team member who can assist in achieving a successful outcome and not as an obstacle to the process."

Even if we have a sincere desire to learn, old habits die hard. As leaders, we need to question our questions. It is very easy when questioning to let our own values, preferences, and biases leak into what we are asking. We must develop the attitudes and skills to notice, analyze, and revise our questions. Before we ask a question, we should preview it in our minds from the other person's point of view to determine whether the question as phrased will be truly helpful. If you are unsure how a question might be taken, be frank and say so. For example, you might say, "I'm not sure how to ask this question, but . . . ?" This is a way of defusing any issue that might arise from the way you ask a difficult question.

Given the realities of organizational life and positional power, it is often helpful to bend over backwards to be clear that you are not seeking a scapegoat. For example, if there has been an accident, rather than come right out and ask "How did it happen?" you might preface your question with a statement like this: "It's important that we analyze every accident to see what factors contributed to it so that we can prevent similar accidents in the future." Once the framework for the question is established, that it is about the future, and focusing on prevention (not about the past, and not about blame or responsibility), then you can ask, "How did it happen?" When you frame the question in this way, the answers you get are likely to be open and informative.

In today's diverse workplace, particular attention needs to be given to framing questions.

Effendy Mohamed Rajab of the World Organization of the Scout Movement in Geneva observes, "Questions, in many cultures, can be threatening if done improperly. Many people are not comfortable when being asked 'why' a number of times, especially in the presence of someone who is their senior. Therefore it is important that you create a positive climate for the dialogue and observe the body language."

In the same vein, Isabel Rimanoczy (an executive coach and a partner with Leadership in International Management) told me, "In Thailand, questions can be seen as challenging the opinion of another person, and rule number one is that no one should 'lose face.' My experience led me to reframe the question as a gift for someone, as a sign of interest and curiosity. This reframing totally changed the perception of the question, and the group easily adopted the questioning process." Framing questions as a demonstration of interest in another person's point of view is helpful in building relationships. It is often useful to frame a question as a gift, as Rimanoczy says. Similarly, it can also be useful to frame a question as a request for a favor: "I value your opinion highly, so I would appreciate it if you could tell me. . . ." In this way, you are asking for a gift rather than demanding something in a manner the other person may regard as improper or threatening.

It is best if the leader frames questions in a positive way, using what Cooperrider (2001) refers to as *appreciative inquiry*. Appreciative inquiry is "the study and exploration of what gives life to human systems when they function at their best" (Whitney, Cooperrider, Trosten-Bloom, & Kaplin, 2002, p. 1). This approach to personal and organizational change is based on the assumption that questions and dialogue about strengths, successes, values, hopes, and dreams are themselves transformational (for both the questioner and the person questioned). It is a relational process of inquiry, grounded in affirmation and appreciation.

So instead of asking what went wrong, the wise leader will tend to ask questions that focus on what has gone well, what could be done, how it could be improved. The approach will guide the group in seeking what might be rather than what is not. The focus remains on improvement and continuous learning rather than complaining and venting. By being open-minded and not negative, the leader encourages fresher and broader ranges of responses.

Timing for Questions

Finding the ideal time for asking questions is an art. If we bring up questions too early in a process, the group or individual may lack the experience to have sufficient data to respond adequately, and thus we may miss an opportunity for understanding. If the questions come too late, we may miss an opportunity for learning and frustrate the participants in the group, who have been struggling without help and support for too long. Experience will make the leader grow more comfortable and confident in timing questions for optimal results.

Steps in the Questioning Process

Asking questions can be and often is a very simple process. Questions often just pop up in the course of a conversation, get answered, and the conversation moves on. When, however, you find that you are confronting a difficult issue, and want to plan things out ahead of time, it can be useful to follow a simple process. First, break the ice and get the conversation going. Second, set the stage for the conversation by explaining what you want to talk about. Third, ask what you want to ask. Fourth, listen attentively to the answers. Fifth, and most important, follow up.

Breaking the Ice

It is useful to start with casual questions to put people at ease and get them talking. As noted in Chapter Four, a simple closed question (Is this a good time to talk?) can often get the ball rolling. Friendly, open-ended questions (How's your day been?) can be used to encourage the other person to open up. Keep the tone friendly as you move to set the stage for your question.

Setting the Stage

As you set the stage, you are framing the question by establishing the context and background for the conversation. Setting the stage is primarily about you, not the other person. As noted, a learning mindset, not a judging mindset, is critical to getting free and honest answers and open conversation.

Be forthright in saying that the purpose of the conversation is to learn, not to judge. It is often helpful to open up yourself, and offer some self-disclosure. You might say something like, "I have been concerned that our sales are not as strong as we hoped" or "I am really excited by this new program we are trying out." The point is to let the other person know where you are coming from. If you are concerned about a problem, describe the problem as you see it as objectively as possible—and let the other person respond to your description before moving ahead. If you are looking for new ideas, say so.

One way to set the stage is to explain what you hope the outcome of the conversation will be. Spell it out, as in the following statements:

> I hope to get a better understanding of why we are having this problem.
>
> I want a better feel for how customers are responding to our new products.
>
> I want to understand how you feel about my plan for the unit.

As long as your objective is learning rather than judging, specifying your objective clearly should not be threatening to the other person.

The key to framing good questions, according to Kouzes and Posner (2002), is to think about the "quest" in your questions. What do you want this person to think about? What do you want to learn? A questing mindset shows that you care about the other person. As the old saying goes, people don't care how much you know until they know how much you care.

The leader should not enter the questing situation with a sole focus on help and advice, as this attitude can evoke defiance, dependency, and defensiveness—all undesirable responses. Asking about how to make things happen instead of focusing on why they don't work is the type of questing that a leader should possess. The impact of questing, unlike that of telling, can be seen if one compares the leadership results of President Carter (who generally knew more than anyone in the room and let them see it) with those of Kennedy or Lincoln.

In his classic *Questioning and Teaching* (1988), Dillon writes that questioning our purpose can be answered by discovering our intent with respect to answers. "Why do I need this information? "What is it that I want to know or find out? What will I do with the answer? How will the answer work to tell or show me what I intend it to do?"

Once the purpose of the conversation is clear, you should move directly to asking your questions.

Asking Your Questions

Make sure your questions are empowering rather than disempowering, as discussed in Chapter Four. Open-ended questions are much more likely to generate a positive, nondefensive response than are closed questions, which offer only a limited range of possible responses. Leading questions will be seen for what they are, attempts at manipulation. "An effective question must be an inquiry," Cindy Stewart of Family Health Council of Central Pennsylvania says. "Too often I have seen people try to embed their solution in their question." She cautions that maneuvering people into accepting a solution is not usually effective. "When dealing with difficult work problems, the more ownership employees have in the solution the more successful the resolution," she notes. These are some of the questions Stewart has found to be most effective:

- How does your solution meet your goals and objectives?
- What are you trying to accomplish?
- What will your customer expect?
- How does this advance our strategic goals?
- How is this supported by our core values?
- What are the factors you considered in reaching this solution?

When asking questions, keep your focus on the questioner and the question, not on the million other concerns you may have. You can't listen and think of the next thing that you are going to ask or say at the same time. The quality of the response is affected not only by the content of the question but also by its manner of delivery, especially its pace and timing. Try to maintain a steady pace. Do not let your eye contact waver. The key to this skill is that you must be genuinely curious and not make the employee feel judged, interrogated, or manipulated. Use verbal encouragers such as "I didn't know that, tell me more; what else happened?"

Questioning leaders are curious. Leaders ask better questions when they are curious rather than demanding. Einstein once remarked: "The important thing is not to stop questioning. Curiosity has its own reason for existing." Seldom do we search or explore for what we already know with certainty. We ask questions about areas unfamiliar to us. The act of inquiry requires sincere curiosity and openness to new possibilities, new directions, and new understandings. As John Wooden, the legendary and highly successful basketball coach, notes, "It's what you learn after you know everything that counts."

It is not necessary to shout or use high volume when asking questions. Oftentimes the more softly the question is asked, the more powerful it is; unlike statements that may be more effective and have greater impact when they are loud and strong. The manner of introducing questions should be gentle and not arrogant.

Try to ask one question at a time. Too often we overwhelm or confuse people by asking several questions simultaneously. Allow for a response before asking the next question. Many of us tend to ask questions one after another to maintain control of the floor, or because we may not be sure if and when we may get the next opportunity to ask a question, or because we have not thought through the question, or because we want to control or manipulate the response to the first question. Such a questioning approach leads to responses of poor quality. People may resist multiple questions, feeling they are at an interrogation. Inexperienced or impatient questioners ask flurries of questions that reveal more of a desire for control than a search for the truth.

Remember that you are engaging in a conversation, not an interrogation, and you should be prepared to be questioned in turn as the conversation moves along. Listen to how you are talking as well as to the answers you get. If you find yourself talking quickly or getting shorter and shorter answers, back off for a time or otherwise slow down the proceedings. Also, you as the leader should be comfortable in reflecting and taking your time in responding to a good or great question that you have been asked. Focus on what is being said so that you fully understand the intent of the question. Pay attention to the words spoken as well as the implied content and meaning embedded in both the content and the manner of the response. It is important to suspend your own preconceptions, associations, and judgments. And be careful not to begin planning your next question. This often requires allowing "wait time" before responding so as to be sure that the other person has really finished.

Leaders should be careful not to rush the responses to their questions. A good question will oftentimes caused the recipient to step back and reflect. A great question will cause even more reflection and silence. Leaders should be comfortable when there is no immediate response to a question. Allow the people being questioned to reflect and let them know that you are comfortable with the silence. Silence tells others that you expect them to respond and to continue. Providing time and silence allows others to dig deeper into their thought processes to answer the question (Leeds, 2000).

Effective questioners understand that not all questions need to be answered immediately. Give people time to mull over your request for information and develop some ideas. The question will continue to incubate in their minds and perhaps a volume of responses will emerge when that same question is asked later. Putting others under a tight deadline inhibits open-minded thinking. Time permitting, it's better to say, "Let's get together in a few days and bounce this around. In the meantime, give it some thought. I would like to have a few suggestions to check out." Remember that the power and value is sometimes more in the question and the reflection that it causes than in the responses that it generates.

If you actually meet resistance, the best thing is to stay quiet. You have to give a person time to think. The person has to process everything about why you are now asking questions and then go through the process of formulating the answer. We sometimes forget or find it difficult to look at the world from a perspective other than our own.

Listening and Showing Interest in the Response

Say thank you when you get a response. This will increase the likelihood that you'll get more and deeper answers the next time you ask. When your questions respect people's thought processes, you support their own questioning of long-held assumptions. It is much harder to ask skillful questions than to give advice. And for many years managers have received positive feedback for having the answers and giving advice. But *our* answers work for *us*. We often need to let others find answers that work best for *them*.

If you are sincerely taking a learning attitude in asking questions, you should not shift into a judgmental mode once you have gotten an answer. Judging or criticizing responses to your questions will only close off learning and innovation. Says Jeff Carew of Collectcorp:

> During my staff meetings I bring up agenda items pertaining to the group's area of responsibility. We may have a customer with a dramatic increase in unexpected volume that requires immediate attention. I will start by asking them to clearly define the problem; then we start listing alternatives to fix our problem. I keep prodding them to give more alternatives and will only volunteer some of my alternatives after I have exhausted all of their alternatives. All of them understand that no alternative is wrong or inappropriate, that we want to get everything out on the table. After the options are out, we then look at the up and down side of each and continue to proceed to narrow them down until we have a basic course of action. This is the way we solve the problems of the day, week, or month.

Peter Drucker and others have noted that the most important thing in communication "is to hear what isn't being said." This obviously requires careful, good listening. Effective listening skills are critical if you wish to get the most out of questions. It is a wonderful gift to have people give you their full attention. It can also be helpful to have people reflect back to you what they heard and felt while listening to you. We sometimes are unaware of our anger or pain about a situation because we have buried the feelings. When the feelings are noticed and reflected back, we have a greater awareness of ourselves. By fully listening to employees without interrupting or leaping in to solve their problems, you set the stage that allows them to find their own answers. Your interruptions, no matter how well intentioned, take the floor away from an employee and put the focus back on you. When you are certain that the employee has completed a thought, then reflect back what you heard and observed.

The executive director for organization development at Novartis, Robert Hoffman, explains why he thinks listening is so important:

> I am reminded of Covey's habit number 5: Seek first to understand, then to be understood. It is important that I listen empathically and try getting inside the other person's frame of reference so I can listen with one purpose: understanding. One cannot truly understand the other person's position without questions. I then work on ensuring, also through questions, that I have clearly communicated my thoughts and ideas.
>
> My staff is most appreciative that I give them the chance to participate as a full equal. I show this by the way I listen to them and trust their judgment. People really appreciate being asked a question and then action being taken as a result of that question.

According to Frances Hesselbein, "We need leaders who practice the art of listening, practice Peter Drucker's 'think first, speak last.' Leaders who are healers and unifiers use listening to include, not exclude—building consensus, appreciating differences, finding common concepts, common language, common ground" (2005, p. 5).

As a leader, you have a number of ways to demonstrate that you are listening to and caring about the person you are questioning:

- Pause at the end of a question so that the answerer can think, formulate, and deliver an answer.
- Once you have asked your questions, listen.
- Use steady eye contact and supportive nods; be alert for "iceberg tips"—body language, facial expressions, gestures, and vague comments that hint a willingness to contribute more information or opinions if encouraged. Staying silent is more than just not talking. It means keeping eye contact, staying still, and feeling comfortable while you wait.
- Be certain to demonstrate that you really want to grasp what is being said. Ask questions that indicate your willingness to encounter and accept new conclusions. Many times it is

necessary to ask clarifying questions so as to assure yourself that you have a complete understanding of the situation.

- Listen patiently, without interrupting. Interrupting may show you are not interested in the response or the respondent.

- Use reflective listening, hearing the words and reading the emotional content.

- Restate what you heard in your own words and ask whether your understanding of the argument is consistent with what was said.

- Voice your critical questions as if you are curious. Nothing is more deadly to the effective use of critical thinking than an attitude of "Aha, I caught you making an error."

- Request additional reasons that might enable the person to make a stronger argument than the one originally provided.

- Ask the other person for permission to allow you to explore any weaknesses in the reasoning. The idea with this strategy is to encourage the other person to examine the argument with you.

- Convey the impression that you and the other person are collaborators, working toward the same objective—improved knowledge and results.

- Show respect for their views by asking open-ended, unbiased questions.

- Focus your listening by asking questions such as "What is useful about this?" and "What can I learn?" rather than "Whose fault is this?"

- Help people learn through the process of answering.

Leaders need to be careful not to interrupt; rather they should make sure they have a complete understanding of the situation. Careful observation and good note taking allows them to be in tune with who is saying what, how, when, and to whom. Active listening requires a great deal of attention. This strong listening enables us to acquire a wider and more holistic view.

Leaders must have a deep commitment to listening intently to others, and thereby become better able to identify and clarify the will of a group. An insatiable, nonjudgmental curiosity will enable a leader to ask the many great questions needed by individuals, groups, and organizations.

Following Up

Following up after a questioning conversation is critically important. Someone who has openly and thoughtfully answered your questions deserves to know what you did with the information. Likewise, someone who honestly responds to a question by expressing dissatisfaction with a process or concerns about a direction will feel ignored if the concerns are never mentioned again. Leaders who do not follow up after posing questions will soon find themselves in difficulties. Cindy Stewart says,

> One important thing I have learned, and try to impart to my executive team, is that a leader who relies on questions alone will ultimately be viewed as insincere and not trustworthy. The power of questions can only be realized through learning, follow up, and change. The leader who asks questions and doesn't pay attention to the answers quickly loses credibility. My use of questions comes from a true desire to learn from my employees. That is reinforced by my efforts to follow up on their answers, which will result in visible changes in process, procedure, or operations.

Executive coach Marshall Goldsmith writes that for leaders, "asking and learning will have to be more than an academic exercise. The process will have to produce meaningful, positive change. By learning how to follow up efficiently and effectively in an extremely busy world, leaders will enable key stakeholders to see the positive actions that result from the input they were requested to provide" (1996, p. 227). When we don't follow up on the responses we get to our questions, others will see our questions as an academic exercise, or worse, as Cindy Stewart says, see us as insincere and untrustworthy.

Alcoa's Mike Coleman agrees that following up—or as he puts it, "giving something in return"—is critical. He says, "It is important that I give them something in return after I have digested their responses to my question. I need to give them information and action, to show the benefit of their responses."

Sincere Listening and Learning

Although this chapter has presented a lot of strategies and techniques for asking questions effectively, the art of questioning is really not about tips and techniques at all. It all comes down to being sincere in wanting to learn rather than blame, in wanting to listen to responses openly and nonjudgmentally, and in following up on the conversation with action. When we are sincere in these ways, the conversation flows almost effortlessly.

6

CREATING A QUESTIONING CULTURE

Knight Ridder, with more than twenty thousand employees world-wide, is the nation's second-largest newspaper publisher, with products in print and online. The company publishes thirty-one daily newspapers in twenty-eight U.S. markets, with a readership of 9 million daily and 12.6 million Sunday. Questioning and learning are an essential part of the corporate culture, and all staff are expected to develop and display the following attributes in building success at Knight Ridder:

1. *Questioning for gathering information:* Use questions continuously for information gathering and analysis. In order to collect information, leaders and employees build relationships and form partnerships with current and potential advertisers, readers, and other information consumers—general market or business. In addition, everyone should be personally involved in community activities or interaction with the community and use that knowledge to inform business strategy. Strategic business knowledge requires continually scanning business and identifying global and market trends.

2. *Collaboration and questioning:* Leaders ask for and hear feedback and data from others that challenge their assumptions and behaviors.

3. *Capturing and sharing learning:* Each person should take responsibility for acquiring and sharing new skills, behaviors, and competencies. Everyone should help to coach others through the development process and share their learnings

broadly throughout the organization. New opportunities and settings should provide new opportunities for questioning and learning.

4. *Nurturing innovation through questions:* Knight Ridder leaders should foster an environment that inspires others to deal creatively with business and people problems. Reward and recognize innovation and develop capacity for identifying effective solutions.

5. *Urgency and questions:* Leaders can demonstrate a sense of purpose by taking prompt action as issues emerge and by pushing for closure and results. Gather and share information while ideas are evolving.

All companies can strengthen their corporate cultures by making them question-friendly, like the one Knight Ridder has. As I noted in Chapter Two, a questioning culture has six hallmarks. When an organization has a questioning culture, the people in it:

- Are willing to admit, "I don't know."
- Go beyond allowing questions; they encourage questions.
- Are helped to develop the skills needed to ask questions in a positive way.
- Focus on asking empowering questions and avoid disempowering questions.
- Emphasize the process of asking questions and searching for answers rather than finding the right answers.
- Accept and reward risk taking.

The Leader's Role in Shaping a Questioning Culture

The goal for the inquiring leader is to change the corporate culture from one of telling to one of asking, to help everyone see and understand that questions need to become their primary communications tool. As noted in Chapter Two, changing the culture of an organization pays dividends. And there is no more effective way of creating a questioning culture than by using questions to do so. "Questions have had the impact of changing the culture from one of employees' feeling disenfranchised to one of ownership," Mark Thornhill told me. As CEO of the Midwest Region of the American Red Cross, Thornhill has adopted a questioning style of leadership. "It has empowered [my team] and caused significant change in attitudes and productivity. It has enabled my manager [and me] to better understand each other."

How can a leader develop a questioning culture? Here are some strategies that can build a powerful learning and questioning culture:

- Start at the top. The questioning culture must begin with the most senior leaders, who model the frequent use of good questions.
- Create an environment that enables people to challenge the status quo, take risks, and ask more questions. Recognize that many standard practices, policies, and procedures are no longer valuable to the company—if they ever were.
- Connect the values and processes of the organization to the use of questions.
- Optimize the opportunities to ask questions by building questioning into every business activity, including formal and informal meetings, sales calls, conferences with clients, or presentations.
- Reward and appreciate questioners; promote risk taking and tolerate mistakes.
- Provide training for people to be better at and more comfortable in asking questions.

Each of these strategies reinforces behavior connected to the six hallmarks of a questioning culture.

Leaders Model the Way

A number of successful leaders have modeled the way in using questions. August Busch III, when chairman and CEO of Anheuser-Busch, encouraged openness in his nine-member board. He insisted that each member come prepared to present an opinion and back it up. When tough issues emerged, he asked executives with opposite points of view to present their perspectives. August Busch attributed much of the success of his company to the questioning and learning culture he developed at Anheuser-Busch (Clemens & Mayer, 1987).

Charles Heimbold, former chairman and CEO of Bristol-Myers Squibb, describes how he built his company into a learning organization. He and other top managers were committed to asking questions—they did not dictate. Effective leaders at BMS, he notes, "know that a good question is much more powerful than an order. They are less likely to tell someone the right answer and more likely to suggest who might have expertise, or who might be available internally or externally for the person to talk with in order to bring the best information to bear on the work" (Heimbold, 1999, p. 180). BMS leaders were constantly walking around asking questions and "looking under rocks." They searched for opinions and ideas extensively inside and outside of the organization. Senior managers were expected to travel and cover a wide range of competitors, suppliers, customers, academics, and other labs so as to get new information and opinions. Leaders encouraged their people to do the same by inviting them to accompany them as well as to go out on their own. The result was that Bristol-Myers Squibb became a vital and stimulating organization, with the kind of energy and electricity that marks a culture that supports innovation.

Chad Holliday, president and CEO of DuPont, is another leader who models the way in his use of questions. In fact, he says, "As I have moved up during my thirty-five years here at DuPont, I have used questions more and more." Early in his career, he says, he was trained "in the nature of questions, and . . . how to ask good questions." Holliday adds, "I tend to ask questions to find out from

others how to shape solutions, how to get alignment more quickly."
He continues:

> Inside DuPont, we have a common and clear objective, so the ques-
> tioning process works well. When our senior people come together, we
> have a framework that guides our discussions. It requires self-discipline
> to keep questioning; there is a great temptation to make statements,
> especially when you are in a hurry and want to do things quickly.
>
> On critical issues, I believe that we must use questions. At our
> meetings, we begin by identifying the three critical questions that
> we need to answer during that meeting. At the end, we ask how
> well we did. The leader of the meeting determines the questions.
> Every meeting has a purpose and should have some final products;
> usually the products are the answers to those questions.

Successful and effective leaders continually search for opportunities to ask questions. When the Center for Creative Leadership
studied 191 successful executives, they discovered that the key to
their success was creating opportunities to ask, and then asking
questions (Daudelin, 1996).

Leaders model the way not only by asking questions but by
demonstrating their willingness to learn and change. Edgar Schein
(2004) notes that leaders must have extraordinary levels of motivation and self-confidence to enable them to go through the
inevitable pain of learning and change. They must also have
the emotional strength to manage their own and others' anxiety as
learning and change become more and more a way of life. Margaret
Wheatley (2002) points out that leaders should be champions of
thinking, reflecting, and open-ended spaces. They must recognize
that their colleagues cannot become smarter by action alone. Great
leaders are eager to see people learn. They understand and appreciate how adults learn and see learning as a way of life.

Questioning leaders can become great teachers and co-learners.
Leaders should look for creative ways to find teaching and learning
opportunities. Through questions, they turn every interaction with
their people into a potential learning event. They often set aside

time to teach leadership outside of scheduled activities. Practicing action learning, taking risks, seeking innovative answers, and asking fresh questions all exhibit solid learning practices and skills to employees. Institutions that succeed over the long term do so because they continuously regenerate leadership at all levels (not just because of their core competencies or use of modern management tools). Questioning leaders strengthen leaders at all levels.

Creating the Motivation and Environment to Challenge the Status Quo

Remember the discussion of Alan Wurtzel in Chapter One? When he first began taking Circuit City on its long journey from near bankruptcy to spectacular growth, he started with a simple admission, *I don't know.*

Successful leaders go beyond asking questions themselves; they work to create an environment in which everyone can ask and be asked questions. This means, first of all, that they focus on fostering a climate where employees feel safe in asking questions and able to trust the system and the people involved. Without this level of safety and comfort, people are generally unwilling to be vulnerable and thus are uncomfortable about asking and answering questions that might seem threatening. And without trust and openness, people are unwilling to communicate about feelings and about problems, so they refrain from asking the leader questions that may help them.

People will not be open to questions if they feel put on the spot in being asked a question. So it is important to be careful in selecting the place and time to ask questions. The leader may need to meet individually at first as some people may prefer not to volunteer opinions in front of a group for fear of criticism. Their questions and responses may be more candid in private. People are often more comfortable on their own turf. Questioning them in their own work setting might put them at ease and will enable them to speak more freely. Later on, they may be more confident and trusting and will be more comfortable in asking and answering questions.

People will also feel on the spot if questions are too abrupt or accusatory—or if an immediate answer is demanded. Remember the guidelines provided in Chapter Five: ask questions out of a genuine desire to learn, in a positive manner, and give people time to respond.

If we really want to create an environment that is safe for questions, we must be committed to the growth of people. People should be seen as having an intrinsic value beyond their tangible contributions as workers. A leader is deeply committed to the personal, professional, and spiritual growth of each and every individual. This includes not only promoting their learning but also taking a personal interest in their ideas and suggestions and encouraging their involvement in decision making. When leaders demonstrate this personal interest, they help create a safe environment for questions.

Leaders can demonstrate their toleration, even encouragement, for challenging the status quo through the use of dialogue. Dialogue is a form of communication that balances advocating and inquiring. Dialogue is based on the principle that the human mind is capable of using logic and reason to understand the world, rather than having to rely on the interpretation of someone who claims authority through force, tradition, superior intellect, or divine right. Dialogue allows the group to tap the collective wisdom of its members and to see the situation as a collective whole rather than as fragmented parts. In dialogue there is an emphasis on asking questions rather than posing solutions, on gaining shared meaning rather than imposing one's own meaning. Dialogue requires trust.

Dialogue involves a relationship built on trusting, caring questions, and when practiced well and often, it builds trust as people see that their questions and observations are appreciated. Central to the concept of dialogue is the idea that through the interaction, people acknowledge the wholeness, not just the utility, of others. The focus is on acquiring greater understanding and attaining shared meaning. As Mark Thornhill says, questions do help the employee culture move from disenfranchisement to ownership.

Isaacs (1993) notes that dialogue is more than a set of techniques for improving organizations, enhancing communications, building consensus, or solving problems. It is based on the principle that conception and implementation are intimately linked, with a core of common meaning. During the dialogue process, "people learn to think together—not just in the sense of analyzing a shared problem or creating new pieces of shared knowledge, but in the sense of occupying a collective sensibility, in which the thoughts, emotions and resulting actions belong not to one individual, but to all of them together" (p. 358). Through dialogue people can begin to move into coordinated patterns of action and start to act in an aligned way. They can begin to see how to fit parts into a larger whole.

When you engage in dialogue, you should make sure every person's ideas are listened to and respected by other members of the group. Encourage participants to suspend criticism and analysis in the process of creatively exploring issues and problems. Respectful listening affirms people's person-to-person relationships and acknowledges the group's collective right and intellectual capacity to make sense of the world. Out of this social sharing of knowledge emerge a common pool of information and the seeds of innovation—new and imaginative insights that may lead to unexpected but valuable ideas.

When we encourage dialogue we affirm intellectual capability not only of the individual but also of the team and organization. We acknowledge that people are all blind to their own tacit assumptions and need the help of others to see them. We make it clear that each person, no matter how smart or capable—and this includes the positional leader—sees the world from a separate perspective and that other legitimate perspectives could inform that view. Wheatley (2002) points out how questions and dialogue have the potential to create "great webs" that help bring the organization together, whereas statements may create more divisiveness for the organization.

Make Sure Values and Processes Do Not Conflict with Questions

Some organizational values may hinder the development of a questioning culture. Some organizations, for example, place a high value on loyalty. Many people interpret loyalty as not questioning anything said by the leader. An organization espousing loyalty as a value needs to be clear about what sort of loyalty it is promoting. Loyalty to the organization, or to the truth, may not hamper a questioning culture. When loyalty is focused on supporting the current leadership, however, a questioning culture may be impossible.

Leaders, through questions, can engage their constituents in a dialogue about values. Ask, Do our values support questions? If not, should we reexamine them and perhaps find more appropriate values? If so, have we really been living our values?

Kouzes and Posner (2002) note that the quest for leadership is also an inner quest to discover who you are. Learning to lead is about discovering what you care about and what you value. On an organizational level, the same is true. Organizations with a questioning culture are on a quest to discover who they really are, what they are capable of, and what they can be great at. Here are some important questions for people in organizations to wrestle with together on an ongoing basis:

- What inspires us?
- What challenges us?
- What encourages us?
- How certain are we of our conviction about the vision and the values?
- What gives us courage to continue in the face of uncertainty and adversity?
- How will we handle disappointments, mistakes, and setbacks?
- What are our strengths and weaknesses?
- What do we need to do to improve our abilities to move the organization forward?
- How solid are our relationships among ourselves?
- How can we keep ourselves motivated and encouraged?
- How prepared are we to handle the complex problems that confront our organization?

- What are our beliefs about how people ought to conduct the affairs of our organization?
- Where do we think the organization ought to be headed over the next ten years?

Asking these questions will help everyone—a team, a department, an entire organization—discover who they really are and what they really value as a group.

A common understanding of values comes about through such dialogue. Organizational values should emerge from a process, not from a pronouncement. If your organization has a formal statement of values, consider engaging people in discussing it, asking how each value affects the organization's ability to develop a questioning culture.

Standard operating procedures can also hamper the creation of a questioning culture. An organization that requires layers of review and approval for even small decisions, for example, is telling employees that they are not trusted to think on their own. These employees know that their views are considered unimportant—and so their questions will be unwelcome.

Optimizing the Opportunities to Ask Questions

We all have numerous and continuous opportunities throughout the day to ask questions. Unasked questions represent windows not opened and viewpoints and vistas not explored—unexploited opportunities to build and strengthen a questioning culture. Leaders who ask questions whenever and wherever they can, have the possibility, according to James Collins, of leading companies from being good to being great.

Too often, we fail to ask questions because we are in a rush. Deliberation is not rewarded in today's organizations, which prize decisiveness and action. When we rush through an agenda at a meeting, or tell people to hurry up with decisions, we are squeezing out the possibility of question. As DuPont's Chad Holliday told me, "DuPont has over six thousand managers, each of whom must make four or five decisions each day. If we can get them to ask the right questions before they take action, DuPont will save a tremendous amount of money and time." Wheatley (2002) suggests that the most important question leaders might ask themselves relate to creating more time for questing with questions such as these:

- How willing are people to work together to get something to work?
- What has happened to my reflection time?
- Are people willing to turn to me when confronted with conflict, grief, pain?
- Where do I see more opportunity for thought?

Sometimes it is easy to find opportunities to ask questions. Says Gidget Hopf of Goodwill: "When someone comes in to see me with a problem or question, I always try to turn it around and ask them what they think about the problem." Most leaders certainly should be asking questions much more frequently and in more situations than they probably are doing presently. Of course, the timing of questions should be based within the context of the situation. Here are some of the occasions when questions are appropriate:

- Problem-solving sessions
- Planning meetings with employees
- Performance appraisals
- Orientation with new employees
- Staff meetings
- Discussions with customers
- Board and organization-wide meetings
- Public and community meetings

Of course, there are many more. Part Three discusses in detail how to incorporate questions into a wide variety of organizational activities.

Reward and Appreciate Questioners

Appreciation has to do with recognition, with valuing and with gratitude. Leaders who build questioning cultures recognize the best in people and the world around them and seek to affirm past and present strengths, successes, assets, and potentials of their people. They look for opportunities to increase the value of the person and the organization. We should thus model a style of inquiry that is constructive rather than criticizing. Leaders who are fully affirmative with their people will tend to be more affirmative in the questions they ask. Such questions will generate more hopeful and positive responses.

While assessing what their employees have accomplished, too often leaders feel they aren't doing their jobs unless they point out the dreaded "areas for improvement." A compassionate and appreciative leadership relationship means allowing employees to make mistakes and learn from them. As competition increases and business environments change, organizations need employees who are willing to learn. To promote learning, employees must be allowed to make mistakes. Fear of being punished for making mistakes will cause employees to play it safe, to avoid risks, and thus to be unable to help the company succeed.

Empathy enables the leader to connect with those questioned. Workers need to be accepted and recognized for their special and unique personalities. A leader should assume the good intentions of coworkers and not reject them as people, even when forced to reject their behavior or performance. Those who find individuals a pain and a nuisance may be respected or feared, but they will not be willingly followed.

Questioning leaders respect each person and show concern for the well-being of all their colleagues. They want everyone to succeed and to learn from so doing. This ability to empathize and be supportive is very important. Leaders should see colleagues and staff as capable of much more than they presently do, of being able to generate "beyond what anyone could imagine." These attitudes develop more trust toward the leader as well as more openness among the group of colleagues and subordinates.

Provide Training in Questioning

Encourage fresh questions by highlighting the benefits of questions and the tragedies caused when questions were not asked (such as the *Titanic*, *Challenger*, and Bay of Pigs stories in Chapter One). Share stories and case examples of how and when questions changed teams and organizations. Present some of the hows and whys of building a culture for questions, learning, and innovation, using this book as a resource. Resource A at the end of the book provides further ideas on training people in the art of asking questions.

Handling Resistance to a Questioning Culture

Creating a culture of asking can be difficult, however, because the corporate telling culture is intangible yet pervasive. As Eric Charoux, executive director of DCDM Business School in Mauritius, told me, "Leading through asking of questions is a culture change that is not easy to bring about—we often prefer to talk with exclamation marks than with interrogation ones!"

The leader who begins to use questioning style and to encourage the organizational culture to welcome and appreciate questions is likely to meet two kinds of resistance. The first comes from people who are taken aback by a leader who starts asking questions more regularly, who are used to having the leader tell them answers instead of ask them questions. These people have *answer dependency*. The second comes from other leaders in the organization who are uncomfortable in adopting a questioning style themselves, who see their source of power as stemming from giving answers. These people have *telling dependency*.

Dealing with Answer Dependency

A leader who begins to ask questions on a regular basis should be aware that people may not understand or trust this new way of operating. If the leader's role has been to solve problems, provide information, and have all the answers, a change to a questioning style will usually cause those who have become dependent on the leader to feel abandoned. They may feel that the leader has some sort of secret agenda, or that the leader is only asking questions to catch them on something. How should one handle these concerns and perhaps skepticism? Clarke-Epstein (2002) recommends that leaders new to using questioning be honest and up-front. Tell those you lead that you have been rethinking your leadership style and that one of the things you are exploring is the value of being a leader who asks questions. This way, listeners are prepared when you ask questions, and you reassure them that you have no ulterior motive. You can also go a long way toward lessening resistance among those with answer dependency by following the guidelines set out here and in Chapter Five.

If you ask empowering questions from a sincere desire to learn rather than blame, give people the time to respond at their own pace, listen to responses openly and nonjudgmentally, and follow up on the conversation with action, then people will gradually learn that they have not been abandoned and that no hidden agenda is in the works. Moreover, if you set the example, provide a safe environment for questioning and challenging the status quo, and appreciate and reward questioners, you will gradually wean people from dependency.

In addition, it is probably wise to move ahead slowly, according to Mark Harper of ConocoPhillips:

> If I were going through this change in leadership style again, there are a few things I would do differently. I made a rather abrupt change in style at the start and went from one extreme of making decisions to the other of asking a lot of questions and making few decisions. The lesson I learned is that a slower change and a better balance might have been more effective.

Dealing with Telling Dependency

For all the reasons discussed in Chapter Three, other managers in your department or organization may see the move to a questioning culture as undercutting their authority. They may have built their careers on technical competence, on being right, and see moving to questions as a direct attack on what has made them successful. Saying *I don't know*, as Alan Wurtzel did, may just be too threatening. Others may resist the whole idea of using questions because they see it as giving up control. Sometimes they fear that questions may bring them unwelcome information.

People don't resist change as much as they resist being changed. In other words, the way to get others to adopt a questioning leadership style is to ask them to do so, rather than tell them to do so. Telling people rather than asking by its very nature lays the foundation for defensiveness and resistance because it does thrust change upon them, and this is especially true when the telling involves informing people how they personally need to change. Why? When we tell someone what to do differently and why it is important to do it, we convey subtle—even if unintended—messages along with the information: "my way is better," "you are weak; your way is wrong." So the inquiring leader will try to get other leaders in the organization to lead with questions by asking questions.

Here are some questions to ask to help others see the value of leading with questions and embracing a questioning culture:

- Would you like people to solve their own problems rather than come to you?
- How do you feel when I ask you questions?
- Why do you think the idea of leading with questions makes you uncomfortable?

Use these and similar questions as a way to engage in dialogue, not to score points or engage in a debate. If you actually meet resistance to these questions, the best thing is to stay quiet. You have to give people time to think. The listener has to process everything about why you are now asking questions and then go through the process of formulating the answer. We sometimes forget or find it difficult to look at the world from a perspective other than our own. We only see what is important from our own perspective, which may not be what is important to someone else. People tend to resist changes that are thrust upon them, while they naturally support ideas and changes they help create. Questions, as I have noted, pull people to a possible future. As leaders, our questions have the power to provide support rather than increase pressure on the individuals around us.

Start the Journey

Perhaps one of the most important roles of a leader, according to Edgar Schein (2004), is to create and build the culture of the organization and the groups within that organization—a corporate culture with values and behaviors, with visions and basic assumptions, one that appreciates quality, risk taking, teamwork, ethical behavior, success, and results. The most effective way to build this culture is derived from the questions asked by leaders—questions that inspire, clarify, energize, and both produce and resolve productive conflict.

All companies can strengthen their cultures by making them question-friendly. Leaders must model the way, promote values that support inquiry, ensure a safe environment that permits challenging the status quo, find opportunities to ask questions, reward questioners, and make training available when needed.

What else should you do to create a questioning culture? Mark Harper of ConocoPhillips says you just take the first step. "My advice to others considering using questions to lead is to start the journey. I have seen significant positive results and would recommend this methodology to anyone."

Part Three

A GUIDE FOR LEADERS ON USING QUESTIONS

7

USING QUESTIONS IN MANAGING PEOPLE

Each question a leader asks can provide a wonderful opportunity for the recipients to become empowered, to do something that they could not do before. Questions have the potential to create confidence, to enhance learning, to develop competence, to engender insights. Questions can move each person in the organization to become a better human being as well as a better contributor to the organization and to the community.

In this chapter, I discuss how leaders can use questions in managing their staff—how they can use questions to strengthen their relationships with their direct reports, help them grow, and encourage action and innovative thinking. I also review the use of questions in orienting new staff members, setting goals and objectives, conducting performance appraisals, and leading staff meetings, among other topics.

Building Relationships That Empower

Block (2003) points out that we, as leaders, can open magnificent possibilities with others when we recognize that our questioning, reflection, and conversation with others are, in themselves, important action steps. Thus, even before and without a response of the person questioned, we have established a significant relationship. Through questions, leaders create a social space where authentic accountability, commitment, and community become a possibility.

As noted in Chapter Four, many leaders unfortunately ask questions that disempower rather than empower their subordinates, questions that cause reaction rather than creation. By asking dis-empowering questions, leaders close the gateway to identifying paths to success. *Empowering questions,* on the other hand, get people to think and allow them to discover their own answers, thus developing self-responsibility and transference of ownership for the results.

But even empowering questions don't exist in a vacuum; they need to be tailored to the individual who will answer them. Different people need different sorts of questions, depending on their personality, style of thinking, skill set, and other factors. Suzanne Milchling, head of the Department of Defense's Homeland Defense Business Unit, says it takes some experimentation to find the right questioning style with people.

> The most valuable questions for me are the ones that get the result I want. It is a trial-and-error event with everyone until I get to understand them and how they think. I use questions to match our thinking styles or strategies. For example, one scientist insists on briefing the general first because he is convinced his work has high-level merit. I agree but ask, "Have you considered briefing the chief first? With his buy-in it will be easier for the general to fund your project."
>
> I ask probing questions because my people want to look good and I want them to look good. The goal is to get them to learn on their own. Whatever they want to accomplish is what I help them do. The questions are the catalysts for learning what's already in their minds. The abstract thinkers, like my son Robert, need to be made aware of the details. Their thinking is in patterns and I want them to understand the "detail" thinkers—the people they may have to convince—the people who think in details and linearly.
>
> The most valuable questions for me are those that turn people to look inward at how they are perceived by others. When I ask some of the employees, "How are you going to do the project?" I get a straight answer. Those I call *direct;* I can direct them to do something and they answer my questions in a direct and linear manner.

For other, more abstract thinkers, I need them to cycle within. Asking questions like "would it be useful to get Jim's ideas first? Would he be able to grease the skids for you?" Getting abstract thinkers to recycle their thought patterns in slow motion and out loud to me and others raises questions within them that they may not have thought of before.

It is the question that was unanticipated and not asked that gets our people in trouble. Thus another valuable question is "What question didn't I ask myself or my employee?"

Questions that stress values can build relationships. Whitney, Cooperrider, Trosten-Bloom, and Kaplin (2002) suggest asking value-related questions such as, "What most attracted you to this company? What has it contributed to you and your life? How can we create more of that quality within this organization?" They also suggest questions they refer to as "best in class questions," that is, questions that demonstrate levels of organizational excellence beyond the reach of other "good" organizations as well as geared to meet high levels of employee satisfaction. For example, "What is it about you and the way you do your job that's best-in-class? What effect do these skills or behavior have on your department? On the organization as a whole?"

Establishing a Coaching Relationship with Direct Reports

Carl Rogers (1961), one of the most influential leaders in humanist psychology, notes that three conditions are necessary if we are to help change the person we are with—genuineness, empathetic understanding, and positive regard. Roger Carkhuff (1969) suggests that three additional conditions—respect, concreteness, and self-disclosure—can further strengthen these interpersonal relationships as well as results. Rogers's observations suggest that in building relationships with subordinates, our questions need to be genuine and demonstrate a learning mindset as described in Chapter Five; our listening needs to be active and empathetic, and we should show appreciation for the responses we receive. Carkhuff's additional conditions indicate that our questions should be empowering and specific, and that we should be expansive and open in responding to questions our staff pose to us.

As noted earlier, one of the most important roles for today's leaders is to serve as coach as well as mentor to their subordinates. Mark Harper of ConocoPhillips says, "I lead with questions in my personal coaching sessions with direct reports." When we ask questions of others in a way that signals that we are partners in a discovery process intended to enrich the whole group, we build strong relationships.

Bianco-Mathis, Nabors, and Roman (2002) have developed a powerful model with the following steps in developing and carrying out this supportive coaching role with individuals we might be leading.

1. Establish the relationship through reflection, learning, honesty, and determination.

2. Analyze the experience via inquiry, advocacy, resiliency, and self-management.

3. Process and seek to understand the feedback.

4. Plan actions via dialogue, reflection, problem solving, decision making, and risk taking.

5. Take action with openness, courage, and commitment to learning.

6. Continuously evaluate progress.

Gidget Hopf of Goodwill explained to me how she made the transition to becoming a coach to her staff rather than just a boss:

> About four years ago I began working with an executive coach who had been very helpful in assisting me to gain increasing self-awareness about how I interact with my leadership team. At that time, my coach

and I began to discuss new ways of interacting, including asking questions rather than telling. I had always been inclined to offer solutions rather than empower people to solve their own problems. I just automatically assumed that if someone was at my door with a problem, they expected me to solve it. Through the coaching I realized how disempowering this is, and how much more effective I could be by posing the question back to the individual with the problem. This took active concentration on my part to practice this new behavior, and a lot of reinforcing by the coach.

What I came to realize is that solving others' problems is exhausting. It is much more effective to provide the opportunity for them to solve their own problems. So instead of jumping in with a quick response when someone would come to me, I began responding this way: "Well, I am sure you have had time to think about this and have your own ideas, what have you come up with?" This type of question is very validating, and lets the person know that I respect their knowledge and experience. I have come to believe that solving people's problems sends a message that you don't think they can do it themselves. Very often people have thought out their answers and just want to test them with someone else. I now give them a chance to do that.

Tom Laughlin of the consulting firm Caravela described three questions that he has found to be especially helpful in building relationships with his staff:

- *How can I help you?* This question has generated some phenomenal responses. It clarifies immediately what the person wants. Oftentimes, the only thing that people want is permission to execute their own strategy. Other times, they may be seeking advice or wishing to inform me.
- *What would you do?* I have found it very valuable to find out how people would respond to their own problem or to their own question.
- *What would someone else (say, a competitor) do?*

Good leaders regard every encounter as an opportunity to coach. A key skill of coaching is the art of questioning. Asking incisive questions inspires people to think, to discover, to search.

Fostering Reflection and Learning

Reflection involves recalling, thinking about, pulling apart, making sense, and trying to understand. Cultivating the ability to reflect can help generate tremendous personal, intellectual, psychological, and social growth. Reflection helps people experience "breakthrough learning" when they became aware of the need to reach beyond their conscious beliefs and challenge their assumptions about their present worldview. Questions that encourage reflection are the key to significant, or what Mezirow (1991) calls *transformative*, learning. Questions enable individuals to gain both double-loop learning (why something occurs) and triple-loop learning (what in the system causes the something to occur).

Reflection increases self-awareness, which helps people relate to others more genuinely. When we ask others to reflect, to look within, it can help us understand them on a deeper level. In other words, when others understand themselves more fully, they can reveal themselves to us in a more robust way. Robert Hoffman of Novartis provides a telling example:

> I remember working with one outstanding person with whom I would struggle over issues and strategies. He had assumptions that were very different from mine. I soon realized how useful it was to ask him questions and to find out about his underlying thinking. I asked questions such as, *What was going on in your head when you did this? What values caused these actions?* These questions led to trust and the development of a good working relationship.

Hoffman was having trouble understanding his colleague. He used questions to encourage the colleague to reflect, which led to Hoffman's having a better understanding of the other person. Of course, a trusting relationship is important when we ask people to reflect and reveal to us the insights they discover.

Whitney et al. (2002) suggest the following questions as very valuable in generating reflection, learning, and career development:

- How do you learn best?
- How did you foster your own development?
- What made this a high-point learning experience?
- What were the most challenging and exciting career development opportunities that you have experienced?
- What made it challenging and exciting?
- How did you benefit?
- How did the organization benefit?

Of course, we need to help ourselves reflect as well. According to James Champy, "Great achievers learn to temper their ambition with self-reflection. They remain true to their values, see the world (and themselves) clearly, and effectively manage the resources that can limit the pursuit of a dream—time, talent, and momentum" (2000, p. 16).

Questions challenge one's programmed knowledge, or what Schein (2004) refers to as "theories in use." Reflective inquiry generates dialogue and mutual support for each other, as questions require us to listen. Bass (1985) points out that changes in attitudes, assumptions, and values require reflection on the individual's own mental models. Without self-awareness of mental models, it is impossible for a person to change.

Encouraging Action and Innovation

Questions transform problem- and possibility-talk into action as they move people from the present to the future. Marilee Goldberg (1998a) remarks how questions are the primary means by which doing, having, accomplishing, and growing are catalyzed—and often even made manifest—in our lives. Because questions are intrinsically related to action, they spark and direct attention, perception, energy, and effort, and so are at the heart of the evolving forms that our lives assume. Mark Harper of ConocoPhillips uses a variety of questions to spur innovation and activity:

- What is a viable alternative?
- What are the advantages and disadvantages you see in this suggestion?
- Can you more fully describe your concerns?
- What are your goals?
- What is the current reality?
- What are a few options for improvement?
- What will you commit to do by when?

To encourage innovation and action, leaders should encourage people to think about their own solutions, instead of giving them solutions to problems. Ask questions such as "What do you think is the real problem?" or "If you proceed in that direction, what are the possible consequences?"

Questions can, as Peter Vaill (1996) observes, open people to the possibility that they are capable of spontaneously generating astonishing new material, material that goes far beyond what anyone imagined was possible. Gary Hamel, chairman of the innovation consulting firm Strategos, says that innovators typically view the world through four lenses: they look for deeply held conventions and challenge them; they look for change in the world and understand the revolutionary potential of the change; they empathize with customers and anticipate their needs; and they view their organizations less like businesses and more like skill sets, constantly asking, "How do I creatively recombine what I know to make new things?" (Hamel, 2003, p. 16).

Questions to Build Leadership

Bossidy and Charan (2002) note that one of the most important roles of the leader is to create the next generation of leaders. As Pentti Sydanmaanlakka, a former HR director at Nokia, said to me, "Leadership is . . . inspiring and showing others new places where they haven't been earlier. Good leadership is showing the way to self-leadership." Frances Hesselbein, chairman of the Board of Governors of the Leader to Leader Institute, agrees: "Building a sustainable organization is one of a leader's primary responsibilities. When the challenges of today have been met, will your organization have the vigor to grow tomorrow?" Two keys to building sustainable organizations, she says, are grooming successors, "not a chosen one but a pool of gifted potential leaders," and "dispersing the tasks of leadership across the organization until there are leaders at every level" (Hesselbein, 2001, p. 5).

Asking questions and helping people feel in control of their own lives is a key factor in creating leadership capabilities within each person. Asking people what they think encourages them to expand their opportunities to develop ideas, to be listened to, to test out actions.

Jeff Carew of Collectcorp told me, "Employees, specifically your direct reports, need to have an opportunity to learn from you—learn everything about your job—if they are one day going to take on more responsibility, preferably some of your current responsibilities, to allow them and yourself to grow."

"What have you done today to develop your leadership skills?" is a question frequently asked by Neal Anderson of TESOL (Clarke-Epstein, 2002, p. 211). Executive coach Isabel Rimanoczy says that she helps people grow and become leaders "by focusing on questions rather than on answers." Too often employees focus on leaders, looking to them for answers, as if leaders were the source of all knowledge. "We put the focus on them, trusting their knowledge and wisdom. And, even when they did not think they had answers, they dived into themselves for the answers—and not surprisingly—they always found the answers." She adds, "A deep transformation . . . had taken place in those individuals because they had increased their self-awareness and realized that there was wisdom inside them that could be unearthed with questions."

Managing Key Employee Interactions

As leaders, we meet with our staff informally quite often. But in addition to these daily interactions in the course of work, we also have more structured and formal interactions, involving new hires, performance reviews, and the like. Questions can make these sometimes bureaucratic sessions more powerful than fill-in-the-blanks routines.

Questions for Planning and Setting Objectives

Leaders should meet regularly with staff to discuss projects, activities, concerns, and issues. Too often these meetings are set up with statements such as "report to me by three o'clock on Friday." In planning and setting objectives, the leader could ask some of the following types of questions, which can all act as springboards to better, more effective action:

- What do we need to accomplish?
- What do you think is realistic?
- How are you planning to accomplish this objective?
- What resources are you looking for?
- What kind of help do you need?

In checking progress toward goals, you can inspire better work by asking your colleague a series of nonthreatening questions such as these:

- Are you still on track to have that report finished by Friday afternoon?

- Do you have all the information that you need?
- Would it be useful for us to go through some aspects of the report?

Such questions cause people to reflect on the goal you are after and also to anticipate what needs to be done. If there are problems or potential misunderstandings, asking nonthreatening questions provides an opportunity to uncover and address potential pitfalls before the action is completed (Goldberg, 1998b).

Cargill's Douglas Eden says,

> Effective questions for me relate to goals. I often ask questions such as What are your goals for this year? What is really driving you this year? What would it look like if you achieved that goal? Discovering one's goals can help one to prioritize, to become aware of inconsistencies among goals, to help develop great relationships.

Leeds (2000) identifies a number of other types of questions that can be introduced during sessions to set plans and determine strategies.

- *To call attention to a point:* Why do you think John found it difficult to accept this challenge?
- *To get information:* What is the best way to get there from here?
- *To uncover causes or relationships:* How has the conflict with Bob affected progress on this project?
- *To test ideas:* Suppose we did it this way? What would happen?
- *To keep the discussion to the point:* Can we go back to [whatever the original focus was]?
- *To bring out opinions and attitudes:* How do we feel about this?
- *To bring out reactions to a point made:* How do you feel about?
- *To suggest an action, idea, or decision:* What do you think the results would be if you did [something]?

Determining the place and time of asking questions of those who are reluctant toward inquiry is important. As noted in Chapter Six, you may need to ask questions in private at first to make things easier for people who prefer not to volunteer opinions in front of a group. After a while, they may become more confident and trusting, more comfortable in asking and answering questions regardless of the setting.

Questions During Performance Appraisals

Performance appraisals have become such horrible experiences for both the supervisor and the employee that they are dreaded by both parties. Most of us would rather skip than conduct these appraisals. The appropriate questions, however, can make these events more productive—even actually enjoyable. Sue Whitt of Abbott Laboratories, who served as senior vice president of Worldwide Development Operations for Pfizer's global R&D business as well as vice president of Worldwide Technical Operations for Parke-Davis, encourages the use of questions in performance appraisals:

> With my staff, I found that questions are equally applicable and essential for improving performance. Questions during performance appraisal sessions can be very powerful as they can be individualized. Through my questions, they could see how their behaviors were counterproductive to what they wanted to achieve.

Clarke-Epstein (2002), in her research on great questions for leaders, received suggestions such as the following, which would be very effective to ask employees during performance appraisal sessions:

- How does your work contribute to our success?
- How could you make your job more effective?
- Who do you see as our competitors, and how do you see them?
- What gets in the way of doing your job?

- What does our leadership team do that gets in the way of your job?
- How could we communicate management decisions more effectively?
- If you could change one thing about the organization, what would it be?
- What's a potential benefit that we could offer that would be helpful to you?
- What is it like to work on a team in our organization?
- What makes you proud to work for this organization?
- What's something you've learned in the past week?
- What brings you joy in your work?
- What gives your life meaning?

Questions such as these might even be given to the employee beforehand so that the performance appraisal becomes a dialogue that results in actions and learnings that benefit all parties—the employee, the supervisor, and the organization as a whole.

David Smyk, who has more than twenty years' experience in major firms, says that there is always one more question to ask: "One of the most powerful questions is one that I ask at the end: *Are there any questions that I have not asked you that I should have asked you and, if so, can we discuss them now?* You wouldn't believe the additional information I am able to obtain in most cases."

Jeanette Partlow, president of the Maryland Chemical Company, says she uses questions like these extensively in performance reviews:

- What is your goal?
- What was your performance?
- Is there a gap?
- What caused the gap (either positive or negative)?

• Based on this information: For next month, to close a negative gap or preserve a positive difference, what will you keep doing, start doing, and stop doing?

Giving Feedback. By the nature of the performance appraisal process, many leaders may feel compelled to give what they fondly think of as "constructive" feedback rather than ask positive questions. If constructive feedback is needed, the best approach is to ask people what they think should be worked on. In most situations, employees are very aware of their shortcomings. When those areas are enumerated by the employee, you can suggest working on the one or two you think would be most beneficial to improve upon. This keeps you in the realm of coaching, not judging. According to Pentti Sydanmaanlakka, using questions is especially powerful when giving feedback:

When giving feedback there are some basic rules, and the first one is that people should first give their own corrective feedback. Usually they are then quite open and critical. Then when you are giving your corrective feedback, you should do it using questions like: "Do you think your performance was optimal in this case? Do you see any ways to improve your performance? What things would you do differently if you would start the project once again?"

People themselves should seek to gain insights relative to their strengths and weaknesses. It is better that they understand them first; they should tell them to you and not vice versa, as is usually the case. Depending on the situation, I have found the following questions to be most effective:

• *Inquiring:* Why did you do it in this way? What should we actually do?

• *Concretizing:* Can you give some examples?

• *Exploring:* Can you say some more about why you have come to this conclusion?

• *Challenging:* Don't you see any other way to do this?

- *Coaching:* What did you learn in that process?

- *Reorienting:* What is actually our problem? Can you find a totally different kind of approach to it?

- *Summarizing:* Can we agree about this? How would you summarize your solution?

Encouraging People to Ask and Respond to Questions. Because of the high-stakes and stressful nature of typical performance reviews, we should not be overly surprised when employees are reluctant to ask questions or uncomfortable in answering questions addressed to them. Your staff also may doubt whether you are truly interested in what they think, and they may fear that their answers may be wrong, dumb, or unacceptable.

Marshall Goldsmith (2000) has found the following advice valuable in getting employees to open up and to ask or answer questions. Goldsmith suggests that the leader have a conversation built around six discussion points, starting each conversation by describing them so that the other person doesn't feel set up or trapped in a game of "guess what the leader wants." Each of these questions can help people understand what you are trying to teach and achieve. Leaders should be careful to consider carefully the impact of each question.

1. *Where are we going?* I will tell you where I think we're going; you tell me where you think we're going.

2. *Where are you going?* I'll tell you where I see you going; you tell me where you see yourself going.

3. *What are you doing well?* I'll give you my sense of what you're doing well; you give me your sense of what you're doing well.

4. *What suggestions for improvement do you have for yourself?* I'll tell you what suggestions I have; you tell me what suggestions you have.

5. *How can I help you?* I'll add anything else I think I can do; you tell me what I can do to help and support you.

6. *What suggestions do you have for me?* I'll tell you what I think I need to do; you tell me what you think I need to do.

When done well, performance appraisals do not have to be exercises in accusation and denial. Questions are the key to making appraisals learning opportunities for both the supervisor and the employee.

Questions for New Employees

Early days on the job are excellent opportunities for the leader to help a new employee feel comfortable in the new environment and have confidence in the organization's leadership, to show interest and commitment to their ideas, and to inspire and encourage the individual to take actions. Some of the following questions would be valuable during these first days:

- Why did you decide to work for us?
- How would you describe our organization?
- What's one great question I could ask someone new (or an old hand, a customer, and so on)?
- What questions can I answer for you?
- What do you need to learn—both in terms of skills and people to know?
- What would you like to be doing in five years?

Clarke-Epstein (2002) suggests that those who bring in new leaders ask them some of the following questions:

- Why do you think we made you a new leader?
- What did the greatest leader you ever had do?
- What do you need to learn to be a great leader?
- How can we support you to grow as a leader?

And when you become a new leader, it represents the perfect opportunity to use your naive understandings to your advantage. At that stage, colleagues are more tolerant of your dumb (or what Revans would call *fresh*) questions. It is easier to ask why the organization does this or that, or to ask employees what really bugs them about the organization. Here's one great question for the new leader to ask subordinates: What gets in the way of doing the best job possible?

A Final Word

Using questions can help you to become a better leader and generate stronger results from your staff. But it has another benefit. Questioning your colleagues can help them become questioners as well, individuals who generate a questioning insight as a way of life. Vaill (1996) points out that self-awareness and astute understanding of personal motives are the most critical of all leadership skills. Enabling and equipping people to become reflective practitioners will help them become better leaders. This readiness to change and grow via questions is a prerequisite for development.

8

USING QUESTIONS TO BUILD TEAMS

Teams now dominate organizational life, from senior executive teams and cross-functional teams to project teams, virtual teams, and more. Peter Senge (1990) remarks that teams have become a critical component of every enterprise, that teams are now the predominant unit for decision making and getting things done. Tom Peters (1992) points out how the critical work of organizations will need to be done in groups—due to the demands of customers, speed, learning, and efficiency. Long ago, Margaret Mead, the world-famous anthropologist, noted that we should "never underestimate the power of a small group with dedication to change the world; it is, in fact, the only thing that does."

But teams are not without their problems. Margaret Wheatley (2002) observes that in too many organizations *team* is a four-letter word. Unfortunately, most groups are ineffective when first formed, and many never improve thereafter. Members of many teams and groups are frustrated by the ineffective productivity of their group and the painful social interactions and storming that occur within.

For many of us, team meetings are emblematic of the problems with teams. Too often, meetings are held with fixed agendas and little time for questions or open-ended discussions. Not much gets accomplished, and agreed-to tasks are frequently not implemented. Communications are strained, one-way, and often overtly or covertly hostile. Even when meetings have a clear agenda, the overall purpose of the meeting can be obscure. All too often team meetings sap energy and enthusiasm when they should leave people feeling energized, with a clear direction and eagerness to move ahead.

In this chapter, I discuss how leaders can use questions to improve team functioning, solve problems, and resolve conflict.

Leading Teams as a Coach-Questioner

Bianco-Mathis, Nabors, and Roman (2002) distinguish between how a traditional leader leads a team and how a coaching leader behaves; that is, between a leader who tells and a leader who questions. The traditional leader focuses on control, seeks to minimize risk, and pushes to be the initiator of action. Such a leader tends to give commands via statements, to control change, hoard information, and foreclose debate. From the traditional perspective, the team exists for the convenience of the leader. The result is a group that achieves limited development, remains dependent on the leader, asks few questions, and accomplishes relatively little.

On the other hand, the leader who coaches with questions sees the team as having an independent existence in its own right, serving a larger organizational purpose. Such a team has the potential to grow continuously. A coaching, questioning leader develops a group which possesses and demonstrates a culture of trust, support, and open discussion. In this type of leadership, the leader reminds people of their capabilities and strengths, and that they are more likely to continue to build their power as a group. Exhibit 8.1 illustrates the differences between these two types of group leaders.

Mark Harper of ConocoPhillips went through two mergers in quick succession. His story of how he put together a team in a difficult postmerger environment illustrates how a coaching and questioning approach can build teams:

> Two years ago, following a second merger in less than a year, I was struggling to get my management team aligned and fully engaged. Following the first of those two mergers, only about half of this team seemed to be truly committed to the new organization and I was looking for a new way to lead my group out of this second merger. At

Exhibit 8.1 Traditional and Coaching Leaders' Behavior and Legacies

Traditional Leader Behaviors with Team	Legacy	Coaching Leader Behaviors with Team	Legacy
Focus on containing and controlling.	Limited development.	Focus on expanding and facilitating.	Team continues to redefine itself and grow.
Initiates action.	Team follows directions and waits until told.	Holds self and team accountable for initiating actions.	Team values keeping promises and performing as promised.
Minimizes risk at expense of timely action.	Bias toward inaction and using only tried-and-true methods.	Facilitates acting with speed and flexibility; pushes for creative solutions.	Bias toward action—team routinely takes calculated risks.
Gives commands.	Team doesn't participate, raise questions or suggest alternatives.	Consults with team regarding problems and solutions.	Team uses a helping stance—recognizes handoff and opportunities for support—learns how to work toward solutions independently.
Establishes boss-subordinate relationship with team.	People are defined and limited by their positions.	Establishes partnership with team.	Team members are engaged and accountable.
Hoards information and knowledge.	Discourages responsibility and trust.	Shares knowledge and information.	Encourages responsibility and builds trust.
Tries to dictate or control change.	Team members display resistance, fear, and poor performance.	Tries to lead and plan for change collaboratively.	Team accepts change as way of life—displays resilience and adaptability.

about the same time I participated in a 360-degree feedback process and received some personal coaching from some consultants who were helping me to initiate a Balanced Scorecard management process.

The coaches introduced me to a method of leadership coaching called the GROW model, based on the work of John Whitmore (2002). The GROW model suggests that coaching is best accomplished through the use of effective questions. Those questions help to focus people on their *Goals*, current *Reality*, *Options* for improvement, and finally on *What* they will commit to do to improve.

The impact of using questions like these has been to get people to open up and put more of their concerns on the table. This has had many positive results. There have been so many positive changes that I am amazed that only eight months after merger closure, it is hard to imagine that we could have accomplished as much in any other way. A few of those changes include the following:

- A more aligned management team
- A clearly defined vision and strategy
- A culture that no longer talks about the "old way"
- An energized organization
- A new business model
- New brand and imaging positioning

The bottom-line impact on the organization includes targeted merger synergies that have been achieved and exceeded, employee morale improvement, reduction in operating expenses, and solid sales volumes during a difficult economy.

Similarly, Sue Whitt talked to me about putting together a new team after a merger between Pfizer and Warner-Lambert:

I asked people to move their personal agendas. Different people were needed to design and develop different parts of our merger with Warner-Lambert. We had to learn how to interact. I remember how we were all looking around at each other at the table. No one knew what roles each would have. I quickly recognized that people were more receptive to using questions. Everyone needed to learn in order to do the task. Being able to ask good questions was essential. As a result of our questioning and collaboration, our bosses were very impressed, noting that the team was so effective, laughing and working—and not fighting like the other teams.

Mark Harper says that he uses questions in four ways in leading his team:

> One use involves encouraging people to see things from a different perspective. Surfacing and changing unconscious biases is very important in a postmerger environment. A second use involves getting all the issues on the table. Many times I have sensed that I wasn't hearing all of the concerns that existed and the careful use of questioning helped me to surface those concerns. A third way that I use questions is to get everyone engaged in important issues, either in meetings or in one-on-one situations. And finally, I lead with questions in my personal coaching sessions with direct reports.

As Harper's and Whitt's experiences demonstrate, a leader can strengthen a team in a multitude of ways by asking questions of the group and encouraging others to ask questions as well. Skillfully using and encouraging questions can help you achieve a number of specific goals:

A shared commitment to solving problems. To help the members realize that they are accountable and that they must work together if they are going to be successful, ask, *How has this problem affected us? What help do we need? How can we improve our communication and collaboration? Who else has something to contribute on this topic?*

Alignment around clear values and goals. To help people jointly clarify the goal and achieve agreement on what the group should do, ask, *What are we trying to achieve? Who has a different view? What's the ultimate purpose behind this goal?* Use questions to remind members not to assume that everyone automatically agrees on the goal of the group, and that consensus on a goal is only possible if they ask questions of each other.

Willingness to work with others to develop strategies. In many groups, the members have been thrust into problems and situations entirely new to them (especially if the team has sought members who may have fresh questions as well as individuals who have experience with the issue). To remind people that no one in the group will have all the answers, ask, *What is marketing's perspective on this? What is manufacturing's perspective? Who else has something to add? How can we bring these different views together? Have we thought of all possible options?*

Improved morale. David Smyk told me, "Don't underestimate how one can also use questions to increase morale. For example, *What can the rest of the team do to help you on this project?* When people know you want them to succeed and you are willing to put your work aside to help them, they tend to perform better and do so with less stress."

Clear and accepted norms. To help establish unique and strong group norms, norms that are powerfully ingrained and provide strong cohesion for the group, ask, *How well are we doing? Are we listening to each other carefully? What is not working in how we deal with each other? How can we improve? Are we excluding ideas or approaches without giving them full consideration?*

Respect for one another and support for one another's ideas. When the leader is careful to ask questions of, and listen to, every member of the group without exception, it sets a powerful example for everyone on the team. To make sure everyone is included, single out by name those who have held back and ask, *Do you have anything to add?*

Improved learning and a willingness to help others to learn. To help members discover how to learn from each other and put that learning to work for the organization's benefit, ask, *Who has had experience with this issue? Does anyone have a different idea? How do people feel about this in your department?*

A fuller understanding of the situation you are facing. Gidget Hopf says questions can provide a useful reality check:

My leadership team met after a particularly difficult board meeting and I went around the table and asked each person: *What did you hear and what did you come away with from that board meeting?* This helped us to clarify and validate what we all felt, and it helped me to see how each individual perceived the discussion. We gained a great deal of clarity without its becoming a whining or bitch session. I will also sometimes throw out a thought and ask people to react. For example, with my senior leadership team, I might say the following: *I am feeling that the team is starting to show some cracks, what are your observations, how do you feel about my observation?*

Encouraging Open Discussion and Debate

As consultant and author Patrick Lencioni points out, "Teams that fail to disagree and exchange unfiltered opinions . . . find themselves revisiting the same issues again and again" (2003, p. 37). Teams that cannot openly debate and disagree cannot learn effectively, and so keep going back over the same ground. Adds Lencioni, "CEOs who go to great lengths to avoid conflict often do so believing that they are strengthening their teams by avoiding destructive disagreement. This is ironic, because what they are really doing is stifling productive conflict and pushing important issues that need to be resolved under the carpet where they will fester." Lencioni stresses that people can feel confident of making a decision with the full benefit of the collective wisdom of the group only after team members have passionately and fully debated with one another.

John Stuart Mill reinforces the importance of vigorous debate in his classic book, *On Liberty*, noting the following benefits of hearing the other side of an issue:

> Though the silenced opinion may be in error, it may and very commonly does, contain a portion of truth. It is only by the collision of adverse opinions that the remainder of the truth has any chance of being supplied.

> Even if the received opinion is not true, the whole truth, unless it is vigorously and earnestly contested, will, by most

of those who receive it, be held in the manner of a prejudice, with little comprehension or feeling of its rational
grounds. Unless widely held beliefs are challenged by
differing opinions, their value is lost.

Asking what others think enhances their participation in whatever decision will ultimately be determined, and consequently
increases support for the decision and reduces the risk that the decision might be undermined by either inadequate consideration or
unexpected opposition. According to Axelrod, Axelrod, Beedon,
and Jacobs, "Meetings require conversations where people can voice
their support *and* their doubts. My ability to say yes is only as good as
my ability to say no" (2005, p. 56). When the leader uses questions
to encourage a full and open debate, doubts can be addressed and
resolved. People can come to agree and commit to a course of action,
rather than just acquiescing in it. Accountability is the willingness
to act in service of the whole; it comes from acts of consent, not acts
of mandate or direction. Commitment is the choice to act as an
owner. Community is the consciousness that we all have a stake in
each other's success. It is our interconnectedness. When we want
to ensure we have everyone's wisdom, everyone's point of view, and
everyone's commitment, skillful questioning is essential.

I discussed the power of reflection in Chapter Seven. Significant
learning occurs as a result of getting the group to reflect; and significant reflection occurs as a result of good questions and debate.
Through the use of questions, leaders can help group members
examine their actions and interactions and thereby improve the
quality of debate and of learning, thinking, and creativity.
The leader's questions should be open-ended and supportive of
diverse points of view. Leaders need to model the listening and questioning skills discussed in Chapter Five. Ask questions that enable
the group to air disagreements, to reflect on how they are doing as a
group, how they can improve, what they are learning, and how their
learning can be applied to themselves and to their organization. Your
enthusiasm for learning and your commitment to helping the group
succeed should be evident to the group.

Energizing Team Meetings

As noted at the outset of this chapter, team meetings too often sap energy and enthusiasm. When you find people sitting around the table looking bored or distracted, get them engaged by asking questions. Remember Chad Holliday's comment: "I find that when someone engages me in a question, it wakes me up. I'm in a different place." Questions, especially challenging ones, cause the group and the individuals to think and to learn. Questions create energy and vitality in the group by triggering the need to listen, to seek a common truth, to justify opinions and viewpoints. Questions generate a dialogue in which everyone begins to leave their individual limitations to find a new wholeness.

Of course, the way meetings begin often sets tone for how they proceed and what will be accomplished. Thus questions can get staff meetings off to a good start. Wheatley (2002) suggests some of the following questions:

- What are procedures that will bring us together?
- How can we listen for what is different (rather than start with fighting)?
- How can our working together be more relaxing and less stressful?

Axelrod et al. (2005) suggest several ways to use questions to engage people and generate energy during a team meeting:

- Instead of selling your idea, ask meeting participants to identify why your idea won't work. Then listen carefully to what people say. This legitimizes the sharing of doubts and shifts the process from selling to co-creation.
- Give everyone a chance to speak by going around the room and asking where people stand on an issue. Many times conversations are dominated by one or two people. Hearing from everyone often shifts the conversation and allows you to bring closure to an issue.

- Separate understanding from agreement. Simply understanding someone's point of view does not mean agreeing with it, but it builds a bridge. Working for understanding means seeing the world through the other person's eyes. When you do this, you build trust and rapport with that person, and solutions become possible where none existed before.

At the conclusion of the meeting, additional questions should be asked to determine what went well at the meeting as well as what could be improved at the next meeting. Unless you encourage and enable the members to reflect on the just-concluded meeting by asking a few questions, little or no learning or improvement will occur—and your meetings will never get any better. At the end of each session, help the group learn by asking some of the following questions:

- How well has this session gone?
- What has the group done well?
- What could the group do better?
- What are we not doing that we could be doing?
- What actions are we going to take as a group next time that will improve our performance?

Also, when you encourage everyone to focus more on questioning and less on statements, everyone more easily becomes involved in the discussions. One person is less able to dominate. Questions during the meeting also cause individuals and teams to be more receptive to adapting, changing, and growing.

Using Questions in Problem Solving

Frank Andracchi of the Constellation Generation Group stresses the importance of questions: "Using questions to solve problems, explore issues, and minimize the influence of different personalities during the problem solving process was extremely powerful." For one learning session with his team, they laid down a rule (from Action Learning, a training program described in Resource A) that team members could only make statements in response to questions. As a result, he says,

> I found the use of questions resulted in a clear definition of the problem and a much more open flow of information as the group could only answer the questions, and by focusing on asking and answering questions, a significant improvement in comprehension of the information presented. I quickly realized that the use of the right questions was a better leadership tool than the traditional trading of statements.

Leaders should deliberately seek a variety of perspectives in solving problems—and the more complex the problem, the more important it is to seek diversity of perspectives. Even though they create some challenges at first, these different initial perspectives are positive and valuable for problem solving and strategy development. Why?

Lencioni points out one reason in the passage quoted earlier. Another reason, as I noted in Chapter Two, is that we generally assume that, having heard about or experienced the problem, we now know and understand exactly what the problem is. And, even more dangerously, we believe everyone else now has the same perception and understanding of the problem. The reality is that different people who hear about or even experience the same problem will in fact discern it and describe it quite differently. This is especially true when we face adaptive problems.

Technical and Adaptive Problems

Heifetz and Laurie (1997) describe two types of problems faced by organizations and leaders today. *Technical problems* are those in which the necessary knowledge to solve the problem already exists in a documented form or set of procedures. Solving these problems requires the acquisition and application of knowledge in an efficient and rational way, applied in what can be described as a Newtonian manner. Technical problems have a linear, logical way of being solved, with precedents within or outside the organization; they are puzzles with single right answers. Technical problems are somewhat mechanical and may require few if any questions, particularly great questions. *Adaptive problems*, however, are problems for which no satisfactory response has yet been developed and no technical expertise is fully adequate. Questions, reflection, and learning are required both to define the problem and to implement solutions. The challenge of the leader in these types of problems is to mobilize people to make painful adjustments in their attitudes, work habits, basic assumptions, and other aspects of their lives, while at the same time learning their way into the creation of something that does not yet exist.

Adaptive problems have no ready solutions. They require people to apply their collective intelligence and individual skills to the work only they can do. Meeting this responsibility requires unlearning the habits of a managerial lifetime, new learning to meet challenges where current skills are insufficient, and capacity to explore and understand the competing values at stake. Adaptive problems are more difficult to define and resolve precisely because they require efforts of people throughout the organization.

Adaptive work is frequently avoided—and the avoidance mechanisms are often unconscious. Reality testing is often an early victim of disequilibrium. Initially, people will apply routine practices for realistically assessing and addressing problems. If these routines do not work, restoring equilibrium may take precedence over the prolonged uncertainty associated with weighing divergent views and facing the need for changing attitudes and beliefs.

Questions, therefore, are needed not just to seek answers, but to induce everyone involved to seek understanding, to respond to what is being asked, to force us to think. The focus is not on a quest for solutions only but also a quest for opportunities to explore and to learn. For purposes of problem exploration and solving, research shows that questions are always more powerful than statements in clarifying, in gaining mutual agreement, in gaining a consensus of perspective (Cooperrider, 2001; Marsick, 1992).

Whether we are facing a technical or an adaptive problem, the obvious (but unfortunately uncommon) first step is first to be sure the group knows what the problem is. Thus different perspectives and the resulting fresh questions become critical for a full understanding of the problem (for example, that it is an elephant), and only when there is agreement that it is indeed an elephant can workable strategies emerge (for example, tapping the elephant's side or offering a treat) that will then enable us to move the elephant. The acquisition of a wide, panoramic view of the problem can be accomplished only by openly and freshly questioning each other and then reflecting on the responses.

Effective problem solving requires an environment that allows for and encourages people to ask dumb or, more accurately, *fresh* questions. We should focus on generating questions and look for the right questions to start with, rather than jumping directly to finding right answers. The right questions will lead us to right answers. Questions help everyone in the group recognize and reorganize their knowledge. As group members are engaged in asking questions of each other, they gradually gain a group consensus on answers and strategies since they now more clearly see one another's perspectives as well as gaining a greater clarity of their own.

When Warner-Lambert was acquired by Pfizer, Robert Hoffman was one of four people chosen in Ann Arbor to provide full-time support to the integration activities. These activities were widely seen as best practice and were documented extensively in the press and academic literature. Hoffman found that the use of questions showed that one problem they were dealing with was not located where they thought it was, in the technical issues of drug development:

> On one project I identified data that suggested we were not as efficient in drug development process as we needed to be. I asked questions relative to possible causes with other people. We determined through a series of questions that the problem was poor team leadership.

Questions changed our entire way of selecting people for team leadership role. Pfizer accepted it totally. In the past, our leaders were good scientists and chemists but not leaders. As a result of our questions, we developed a new competency model.

Through questions, the group carefully determines whether solving the original problem really resolves the situation. Gaining clarity and consensus on the real problem is thus the first and most important part of problem solving, for if we jump for solutions too soon, we may end up solving the wrong problem. Designing a new drug development process would not have helped Hoffman.

Stages in Problem Solving

Daudelin (1996) points out how questions can and should be asked at each stage of the problem-solving process for the purposes of obtaining information, getting reflection, developing insights, and applying knowledge and learning to future actions. Questions are used to open up possibilities, to clarify meaning, and to structure the progression through the four stages of problem solving. Specifically, she identifies particular types of questions that may be most beneficial at each stage of the problem-solving process.

- *Problem articulation and reframing:* What questions are best at this stage; they allow the group to gather details and descriptions of the situation and help members understand the real problem and thus reframe it in a way that everyone can agree upon. For example, *what* is the most import thing . . . ?

- *Problem analysis stage:* At this stage *why* questions are most helpful; questions such as *Why* is that important? *Why* do you think it happened? *Why* were you feeling that way?

- *Hypothesis generation or diagnosis stage:* How questions allow the group or individual to begin to formulate a tentative theory to explain or address the problem: *How* is this situation similar to or different from other problems? *How* might you do things differently? *How* could we intervene?

- *Action stage:* At this stage, the group may be seeking to describe behavior (test for different behaviors) or to share inferences (test for different views); *what* questions become important again. *What* are the implications of all this for future action? *What* should you do now?

Bianco-Mathis et al. (2002) present a slightly different model of the problem-solving process, as shown in Exhibit 8.2. Their model also includes suggested questions for different stages.

Exhibit 8.2 Questioning via Dialogue

What to Do	*Questions to Ask*
State your assumptions: "Here's what I think, and here's how I got there."	
Ask for input.	Do you have different information?
Encourage different points of view.	Does anyone see it differently? How else could we look at this? What other options could we consider?
Explore others' reasoning.	What leads you to think that? What factor contributes to that conclusion?
Invite them to present their data.	Can you walk me through that so I can see how you got there?
Check your understanding.	Am I correct that you're saying . . . ? Does this mean that you would like to see . . . ?
Link their view and yours.	
Identify a larger context or meaning.	How will this affect our stated commitment to preferred vendors? Can you describe how this might look to our customers?
Work for agreement on steps for moving forward.	What can we build on here to meet our objective? How can we use what we've identified to achieve our goal? What can we do next to move this forward?

Source: Adapted from Bianco-Mathis et al., *Leading from the Inside Out* (2002, p. 71).

As teams go through the problem-solving process, questions can help them move from one stage to the next. Robert Hoffman explains how he uses questions for this purpose:

> In a research-based organization like Novartis, our people are outside the norm in terms of raising questions at meetings; they are more prone to be investigative and it is more difficult to gain closure and integration. I have discovered that the best way to reach closure and consolidate our thinking is to ask questions and to check out what I have heard. *This is what it sounds like; am I correct? What are the options? What should we choose?*

Helping the Team Overcome Obstacles

At any stage of the problem-solving process, a team can get stuck, not seeing a way forward. When a team gets stuck, the members often wait for the positional leader to make a statement, define a problem, or propose a solution. Team members hold back, waiting for the leader to accept responsibility. The wise leader will not fall into this trap. The use of questions is an effective way to keep responsibility where it belongs, as Sue Whitt demonstrated with her team: "When projects were off track, I asked them to think of times they made that choice and why. This got them thinking and speaking. I would ask, 'Why did you take this path? How does this connect to the goals set?'" Whitt's questions prodded her team to accept responsibility for grappling with issues.

To help shake things up so that the team can see things from a new perspective and move forward, it's useful to ask the following types of questions:

- *Open-ended questions:* Unlike closed questions, which seek a short, specific response like yes or no, open-ended questions encourage people to expand ideas and allow exploration of what's important to them or what is comfortable for them to reveal. Asking open-ended questions also encourages them to do the work of self-reflection and problem solving rather than justifying or defending a position. For example: *What do you think about . . . ? Could you say more about . . . ? What possibilities come to mind? What might happen if you . . . ?*

- *Clarification questions:* When someone is not clear or you do not experience a full understanding of a situation, you might ask the person to define or explain the statement. For example: *Let me see if I am clear. Are you talking about . . . ? Are you saying . . . ? Could you say that in different words?*

- *Questions for details:* When someone is not clear, you may ask for further bits of information. For example: *More specifically, what are some of the things that you have tried? Have you asked so-and-so what his major concerns are? Does thus-and-such agree that there are performance problems?*

- *Stimulating questions:* Introduce ideas and options by asking questions rather than suggesting a course of action. Emphasis is on asking, rather than telling, inviting a thoughtful response and maintaining a spirit of collaboration. For example: *Let me see if I am clear. Are you talking about setting goals based upon your feedback?* This implies that person should use feedback as a guide to setting goals. Similarly, *have you asked so-and-so what his concerns are?* can be used to offer someone the option of inviting so-and-so to speak about his priorities.

- *Probing questions:* Go below the level of events and behaviors to search for internal drivers that trigger a person's behavior. For example: *Why did this happen? Why did you believe this would be the result?*

- *Summarizing questions:* Invite others to complete or end the discussion with questions that capture the key issues or action. For example: *What is the major point that has been made here?*

Charles Ostlund, principal of Oakton High School, tells of his approach with teachers who seem stuck:

My favorite question to ask teachers who are dealing with an unsuccessful student is, "What did you do next, or what else did you try, or . . . and then what?" Although annoying at times, it suggests that we are always along some point of a continuum of possibilities and whether we choose to move further along the continuum is, in fact, a choice, oftentimes limited only by the questions we choose to ask.

Although Ostlund is talking about helping individuals get unstuck, his approach applies equally well with teams. Whether we allow ourselves to become stuck is, as he says, a choice.

Questions Help You Manage Team Conflict

Conflict around ideas is natural, healthy, and to be expected as teams are organized so as to gain benefits of multiple perspectives. Conflict is an integral part of the team process. Team members with multiple perspectives will inevitably view issues differently and should seek to learn from each other in the process of resolving these differences. Healthy conflict is focused on task issues over which there may be legitimate differences of opinion; or differences in values and perspectives, or expectations about the impact of decisions (Levi, 2001). Questions are the mode of healthy group conflict.

Conflict becomes unhealthy when it involves competition over power, rewards, and resources; when communications are faulty or personal grudges intervene; when team meetings are poorly run; when individuals seek to make individual goals take precedence over group goals. Statements are the common communication mode of unhealthy conflict.

What are some questions that a leader can employ when managing team conflicts? How can we develop trust and rapport among the participants? Ury (1993) suggests the following questions:

1. How can we separate the people from the problem—diagnose the cause of the conflict.
2. What goals are in conflict?

3. What does each side want?

4. Do all sides have a clear understanding of the issues?

5. How can I encourage them to view the conflict from the other side's perspective and to practice active listening?

6. What are the common areas of interest?

7. What are the issues (not what is each side's position)?

8. How can each side get what it wants?

9. What are the issues that are incompatible between the two sides?

10. What are the most important goals of each side?

11. How can we generate options that can be used to solve the problem?

12. What objective criteria will we use as a basis for our decisions?

13. How can we disagree in an agreeable fashion?

Eric Charoux is a partner at De Chazal Du Mee and executive director of DCDM Business School in Mauritius. He provides an insightful analysis of the power of questions in dealing with conflict. "Asking questions," he told me, "transforms conflict into confusion." When we focus rigidly on our own point of view, we cannot see another's. Questions about our point of view can help us become confused, and in that state, we become open to looking at other possibilities. When the team as a whole becomes confused, it is ripe for exploring new possibilities.

Sharing Responsibility

As noted in Chapter Two, when we ask questions of others and invite them to search for answers with us, we are not just sharing information, we are sharing responsibility. Teams are all about sharing responsibility. While a traditional leader may see a team as merely a convenient vehicle for command and control and withhold information and responsibility, the leaders I have interviewed know that this is no longer effective in today's world. Teams function best when responsibility is shared, ideas are shared, problems are shared, and ownership for results is shared. Helping everyone on the team become a better questioner is thus an important way to improve teamwork.

9

USING QUESTIONS TO SHAPE STRATEGY AND ENABLE CHANGE

When leaders shape corporate vision, purpose, and strategy, their focus must turn outward and the questions they ask must go far beyond the company's walls. Questions involving corporate strategy are questions about how the organization relates to the world around it: what markets it competes in, what customers it serves, what alliances it pursues with partners, how it produces its products and services and outsources work to vendors, and how it relates to the community and other stakeholders. Vision and values also must look outward—for while we cannot look to others to tell us what our values should be, our values must be informed by the perspectives of outside stakeholders and relevant to the challenges we face. In this chapter, I explore ways to use questions to shape strategy and promote change, focusing on questions with both internal and external stakeholder groups.

Using Questions to Bring Fresh Perspective

People can easily become entrapped in the organization's accumulated knowledge and established procedures. As leaders, we must periodically question the collective wisdom of the organization. We need to be able to question assumptions about structures, strategies, values, and business processes that shape an organization's culture and operations. In addressing strategic issues, a fresh perspective is absolutely essential if the organization is to perceive new opportunities, uncover hidden and potentially threatening trends in the marketplace, and create new business models.

When Kevin Sharer became CEO of Amgen, he interviewed the top hundred executives at the company, even though he'd already been president for eight years. "Whether or not you are new to the company, you have to bring a new set of eyes," he told the *Wall Street Journal* (Hymowitz, 2004, p. B1). He asked each executive these five questions:

- What do you want to keep?
- What do you want to change?
- What do you want me to do?
- What are you afraid I'll do?
- What else do you want to ask me?

Together, Sharer and his top executives agreed to a new vision for the company, to make Amgen "the best therapeutic company" as it expanded its market beyond dialysis to more competitive drug markets.

Questions can open up new possibilities for virtually every organizational goal and function, be it the understanding of emerging markets, the gathering of information, the building of key relationships, or thinking objectively, learning, or developing an organization. Deep questions about structures, strategies, and values function as openhanded invitations to creativity, "calling forth that which doesn't yet exist." Thus, as Adams noted in a recent conversation with me: "The springboard to every discovery can be understood as the right question, asked at the right time, in the right way, and to the right person(s)."

Questions about strategy, vision, and values should not be treated as technical problems—but as adaptive problems, as discussed in Chapter Eight. In dealing with adaptive problems, we need to provide a forum for active debate and drive the organization to find new questions rather than easy answers. We do this by developing a questioning culture throughout the organization, as described in Chapter Six. To recap briefly, leaders must be willing to say *I don't know* and model the frequent use of questions. We need to encourage everyone in the organization to challenge the status quo, take risks, and ask more questions—and reward those who do. Offer training on effective questioning, problem solving, and teamwork to back up exhortation with resources and action.

Questioning Stakeholders Outside the Organization

The importance of questioning people outside the organization has continued to grow as companies become ever more dependent on such partners within and outside the business chain for information, business, resources, and collaboration. The demarcations between management and employees, between departments and units, between employees and customers, between the company and its vendors, and even between the company and its competitors have become less permanent and more flexible.

Empowering and enabling these various groups of people through questions extends and strengthens the organization. Asking questions outside the organization and outside one's culture may be a difficult challenge for a leader; however, such questions not only cannot be avoided, they must be welcomed, as the responses they acquire from outsiders may serve as the key and impetus of a leader's ultimate success.

Leaders at all levels, including senior leaders, need to create opportunities for asking questions of individuals and groups outside the organization—customers, business partners, suppliers, community groups, and academic and training institutions. Questioning such groups is often vital to the long-term success of the enterprise. Several years ago, Michael Hammer chronicled a number of corporate successes and failures that had occurred in the global marketplace (Hammer, 2001). He examined why Wal-Mart overcame Sears, why Pan Am, the leading global airline of the mid-twentieth century, became extinct, and why Howard Johnson was beaten by McDonald's, Burger King, and KFC. All these failures, he concluded, shared one underlying cause—leadership did not ask the probing questions that might have led them to challenge their basic assumptions, to refresh their strategies, and to fundamentally change their ways of operating. Such questions might have prevented the decline or death of these companies.

Peter Drucker says that in shaping our organizations for the future, we must look at society and community by asking these questions:

> What changes have already happened that do not fit "what everybody knows"? What are the "paradigm changes"? Is there any evidence that this is a change and not a fad? And finally, one then asks, "If this change is relevant and meaningful, what opportunities does it offer?" [Drucker & Maciariello, 2004, p. 367].

Questions for Customers

Many companies recognize the importance of corporate leadership asking questions of their customers. Senior executives of Motorola, including the CEO, meet personally and on a regular basis with customers to ask about the company's services and products. Worthington Steel machine operators make periodic trips to customers' factories to discover their needs via questions. They actively seek feedback, suggestions, and consultation with customers and suppliers.

Canadian Imperial Bank of Commerce (CIBC) is very familiar with the critical importance of learning about their customers through ongoing questions. The bank and everyone in it recognize that they need to know more about the customers and their individually evolving needs. For business customers, it means understanding their industry and their strategy and agenda, and providing solutions to their problems rather than selling previously defined products and services. The process works both ways; customers also need to know more about what banks can provide. For example, derivatives are a complex and valuable set of risk management tools, but often not well understood, even by sophisticated corporate finance managers.

Although asking questions of customers is of course useful for finding out how your company is currently doing with them, an even greater benefit can be derived from using questions to create the future together. Rather than focusing just on how current products and services are meeting customer needs, effective leaders focus on the customers' goals and aspirations. Douglas Eden, president of Cargill's Malt Americas unit, explained to me how he does this:

> I use questions to explore, discover, and create solutions. We wish to be seen as a solutions company which is able to create meaningful value to ourselves and to others. Asking questions of the customers is more powerful for Cargill than selling what Cargill does. As a result, we have systematically built questions into our conversations with customers, questions such as: "What are your goals? What is holding you back from achieving these goals? What are consequences of not achieving your goals? What have you tried to overcome these obstacles? How much is the problem costing the business? In your opinion, what would be the ideal solution for the issue?"
>
> When I first began leading at Malt Americas, we were a business that was losing money. I needed people who were willing to take risks, have self-confidence, and ready to buy into a new vision. Now, four years later, we are a successful business. I attribute much of this success to our ability to ask questions—and to our customers, who were willing to answer our questions. Our business is very complex, and we have to search for the answers together.

By focusing on customer *needs*, Eden was able to turn around a faltering enterprise. And by focusing on customer *goals*, Eden is able to go beyond improving today's business to building tomorrow's. Of course, that is a large part of what strategy is all about.

Customers will more and more determine how organizations set strategies and carry out operations. Customers rather than workers will become the focus of leadership attention and organizational priorities. On a worldwide scale, customers will continue to push for new performance standards in quality, variety, customization, convenience, time, and innovation. Top leadership at Milliken, a large textile and chemical manufacturing company located in Spartanburg, South Carolina, clearly recognize the importance of questions in encouraging and supporting the customer's expectations of improved quality, new innovations, and quicker speed. Milliken staff, for example, accompany the first shipment of each of the company's products to see how it is used and exploit these opportunities to ask questions aimed at finding further product improvements.

Jeanette Partlow, president of Maryland Chemical Company, recognizes the importance of using questions in reaching customers and shaping strategy:

> My company, my coworkers, and I use questions to deliver absolute customer satisfaction and build customers for life. In pursuit of this mission . . . we use questions to conduct customer, supplier, employee, market, and economic assessments that we use in our business and strategic planning. We use questions to problem solve and troubleshoot. We use questions to innovate.

In *78 Important Questions Every Leader Should Ask and Answer*, Clarke-Epstein (2002) has identified several questions that she considers the most critical to ask customers:

- Why do you do business with us?
- Why do you do business with our competitors?
- How and when have we made it hard for you to do business with us?
- What will you need from us in the future?
- If you were me, what's one thing you'd change about my organization?
- What's the most effective way to tell you that we are grateful for your business?
- Suppose this organization could choose just three things to do more or differently to dramatically enhance our customers' loyalty—what would they be?

Leeds (2000) notes that sales requires a series of questions designed to uncover needs and wants, to build relationships, and to foster commitment. Thriving organizations create and maintain exceptional levels of customer loyalty. Loyal customers are great customers. Loyalty, however, is something we must earn. How do we get such loyalty? The best way, according to Bell and Bell (2003), is by asking questions and listening to what our customers want, and, whenever possible, exceeding their expectations.

Research shows that successful salespeople ask up to 58 percent more questions than unsuccessful ones do. Employees on the front lines, be it in sales or service, realize that they can only succeed to the extent that they have knowledge about the marketplace. And their most important knowledge about the individual customer can only come from the questions they ask those customers. Conversations and information gathering from customers provide up-to-date product information, competitive comparisons, insights into changing preferences, and immediate feedback about service and patterns of use.

Questions for Vendors and Partners

The growing presence of global competition and virtual organizations has drastically increased the number of short-term alliances formed between and among companies. Most companies use alliances for the purpose of increasing profits and market share as well as for cutting expenses, time, duplication, and politics. Inquiring leaders, however, seek to add another very important, long-term benefit to the alliance—learning.

Perceptive leaders quickly realize that their success depends heavily on the success of the company's entire business network, not just its employees and customers but also its suppliers, vendors, and partners. Manville (2001) notes how organizations need to embrace the extended enterprise. Organizations have become more virtual through such mechanisms as outsourcing, core competency focus, and the host of alliances, joint ventures, and partnerships affiliated with every company. People, be they employees, contractors, partners, or suppliers, must now work together in value chains to deliver the needed goods and services to customers. Although the links among the pieces of the chain are contractual, they are also defined by exchanges of knowledge, values, and other intangibles.

Questioning (and learning from) partners and vendors has become a critical process across all types of organizations today. Having others in the business chain collectively learn about commitments and policies as well as appropriate management or technical skills can be very valuable to everyone's long-range fortunes. Resources available from vendors and partners, including the gaining of intelligence and competencies via questions, can be critical for the survival of the company. They can also provide competitive advantage.

"Questions are very valuable with technical suppliers and software vendors at Pfizer," Sue Whitt says. "We needed to be and were leading edge by design and were willing to pay the price for what would provide competitive advantage. My questions with vendors and suppliers were more direct. Why are you not doing what we requested? How can we make this work? What can make this faster? How can we get better consultants? How are we going to get it *done?*"

According to Booz Allen Hamilton consultants John R. Harbison and Peter Pekar Jr., companies that are successful alliance builders "reach out for knowledge and expertise. . . . They know from experience that learning counts—and counts big. They set up systems and processes to transfer alliance learning and experience to key managers and hold training sessions and workshops. They also create repositories of knowledge to be tapped into." Harbison and Pekar cite Oracle, Xerox, IBM, Hewlett-Packard, Motorola, Merck, and Johnson & Johnson as successful alliance builders, each having formed more than a hundred alliances.

According to Harbison and Pekar:

The important question is no longer, "Should we form a strategic alliance?" Now the questions are:

1. What types of arrangements are most appropriate?

2. How do we successfully manage these alliances?

3. Are we learning from the experience of ourselves and others? [1998, n.p.].

Up front, at the very beginning of the relationship, the leader should consider what learning is possible from the alliance—customer intelligence, process, and operations policies, cultural nuances, and so on. You may even want to build these learning objectives into the agreement. Leaders (and their learning companies) then should provide an adequate exchange of personnel to be sure to capture and bring the learning back. The alliance provides valuable learning and therefore becomes a rich, long-term investment and profit center that can be used as a basis for future successes.

In forming partnerships and alliances, all parties need to come to clear understandings—and asking the right questions is critical to that process. Stuart Kliman, a founding partner of Vantage Partners LLC, a Boston-based consulting group that specializes in relationship management and strategic alliances, has firm views about the proper procedure at the beginning of any partnership, as *Fast Company* reports:

"Get key people in a room together, and answer these questions: What's our relationship vision? How should we work together to meet our objectives? What challenges will we likely face given our particular business context, the current economic conditions, and our differing strategies?" Kliman says. "Figure out all the challenges that will make it difficult to work together: How are we going to manage conflict? How are we going to handle surprises? How are we going to deal with breakdowns in trust?" Also, determine how those messages will be communicated to the rest of the organization [Tischler, 2001, n.p.].

Companies need to reach out to other parts of their business network as well, bringing partners, contractors, suppliers, and vendors together in an overall learning environment with core employees. Unfortunately, many companies do not reach out for knowledge and expertise to suppliers and vendors, according to a recent study by Bain & Company. "Of those running supply-chain initiatives, fewer than 10 per cent reach out across their network of leading suppliers. Bain found almost 80 per cent of companies' efforts were focused inside their own four walls. How can a supplier fine-tune its production schedules for the customer's benefit if the customer will not share detail on its own forecasts?" (Cook & Jackson, 2001, n.p.). The authors of the study exhort leaders to "reach past your four walls."

Chad Holliday, DuPont's CEO, agrees, saying, "We need to ask all the stakeholders questions, those who supply DuPont, buy from DuPont, sell for DuPont." Companies can share learning with their network in many ways. For example, companies can use certifications to qualify not only their own people but also their partners and suppliers. Ford Motor Company, for example, asks questions and uses the learning from those questions to ensure appropriate procedures, technical expertise, and brand management among its dealerships. Anheuser Busch asks questions to determine the training needed for distributors in the handling of food and beverage products to maintain quality and brand. Cisco, through its constant questioning, is creating higher customer satisfaction and support for faster product rollout by offering learning programs and tools to its channel partners, who provide 70 percent of revenue. Toyota pioneered the use of questions and learning in qualifying and aligning its suppliers; and the "work with us, learn from us, teach us" principle now governs thousands of manufacturing and supplier relationships around the world.

Questions for the Community

A leader who leads with questions quickly recognizes the many benefits that accrue from involving the community as a part of the questioning chain, benefits such as the enhancement of the company's image in the community, the generation of greater community interest in working for or buying from the company, the strengthening of the quality of life in the community, the preparation of a future workforce, and the opportunity to exchange and share community resources. In addition, in working with local schools, the leader may be able to create a win-win situation; that is, allowing teachers and community leaders to participate in corporate training programs and allowing employees to become tutors or resources for teachers and students in the classroom. The local institutions, in turn, can jointly sponsor learning events with the company.

James Austin of the Harvard Business School says community involvement by business leaders is too often "the invisible side of leadership" (1998, p. 38). This is unfortunate, in that leaders who are visible and accessible to the community and the media can be more effective spokespersons for the organization. Relationships between business, the community, and government are often particularly fragile and can easily fray. Leaders who are out of touch with community sentiment and values often step on toes without even realizing it.

In asking questions of community leaders, we should adapt a learning mindset with the aim of understanding their values, concerns, goals, and aspirations for the community. These are just some of the questions you should consider asking:

- How do you feel about our company?
- What can we do to help make our relationship with the community better?
- Is there something you think we do that we should stop doing?
- What do you want us to start doing?
- What sort of information would you like us to provide about the company?

Just as important—if not more so—is making yourself available to *answer* questions from the community. People can be suspicious of business, and being reluctant to answer questions openly and forthrightly often reinforces the feeling that you have something to hide. No doubt some questions will be accusatory and others will be designed to promote an agenda. You will still want to try to answer openly and display a learning mindset as described in Chapter Five. By demonstrating a learning mindset yourself, you can encourage others to move away from a judging mindset.

Developing Strategic Vision and Values

Once your company has gained a full picture of the current reality by asking questions of all stakeholders, it has the context it needs to begin talking about its vision for the future and the values that will help guide it there. Effective visions are developed through conversations, not lamination. They are motivated by relationships generated through the leaders' questions. Seeds of change and future possibilities are created through the questions that leaders ask.

Questions can also build corporate *values*. Questions are fateful; they create a conversational agenda, which in turn becomes the context for envisioning and enacting the future. The more positive the question, the more positive will be the potential for transformation.

What then are some of the questions used by leaders to build corporate vision, purpose, and values? Ken Blanchard, noted author of books such as *The One-Minute Manager, Full Steam Ahead* and *The Secret: What Great Managers Know—and Do*, has identified five key high-level questions in determining the direction of the organization. First, to determine the *purpose or mission* of the company, the leader should ask, What business are we in? The *image* or picture of the company can be developed by responding to the question, What will the future look like if things are running as planned? The *values* of company are determined by the question, What do we stand for? *Goals* are determined by What do we want people to focus on now? Blanchard then emphasizes the asking of the *ethical* question: Is it legal, fair, and does not hurt self-esteem? (Blanchard & Stoner, 2003).

Peter Drucker, after studying organizations and leaders for more than fifty years, discovered that the effective leaders he had met, worked with, and observed behaved in a very similar way. They started out by asking, "What needs to be done?" Then they asked, "What can I do and should I do to make a difference?" They constantly asked, "What are the organization's mission and goals: What constitutes performance and results in this organization." They were not afraid of strength in their associates. They also asked, "What in my organization could I do that would truly make a difference?" and finally, "How can I truly set an example?" (Hesselbein, Goldsmith, & Beckhard, 1996).

Marilee Goldberg (1998a) advises leaders to ask some of the following questions when considering organizational vision and strategy:

- What options have we considered, have we not considered?
- How can this be the best possible win-win?
- What limitations might we be placing on thinking, planning, or actions?
- How else can we think about this?
- Are we being honest with ourselves?
- What's useful about this?
- What can we learn about this?
- How can we make sure we stay on track?

Hewlett-Packard Laboratories recently asked itself, "What would it mean to be the world's best industrial research lab?" The company quickly saw how a big, strategic question galvanized the organization. The director of HP Laboratories began sharing this question with lab employees around the world. She encouraged organization-wide webs of inquiry and conversation, asking people what WBIRL (world's best industrial research lab) meant to them, what it would mean personally for their own jobs, and what it might take to get there. She invited the entire organization to join in exploring the question, first through informal, ongoing conversations and then by way of a more formal internal survey and communications infrastructure. The conversation continued for several months. A creative "reader theater" piece, which reflected eight hundred survey responses detailing employee frustrations, dreams, insights, and hopes, was then developed. Players spoke the key themes as voices of the organization with senior management listening. Project directors helped the parts to see the whole, and the linking of people with complementary ideas together.

Robert Knowling Jr., who has served as CEO of Internet Access Technologies and Covad Communications, says that he uses questions about the future to shape the organizational vision: "Thinking about what future success looks like is the catalyst for visioning" (2002, p. 179). Some of the questions Knowling uses include:

- How successful will our business be?
- What will the corporate culture be like?
- How will the business be viewed in the industry?

Leading Organizational Change

When we use questions to engage the organization's stakeholders and shape our strategic vision and values, it often becomes apparent that the organization needs to change in ways large and small. Pursuing a new vision and a new strategy cannot be accomplished by following the business-as-usual approaches that worked in the past. So, in many organizations, leaders put together a program to sell the changes needed to the organization. This approach usually meets strong resistance.

John P. Kotter, an authority on leading change, says, "According to most assessments, few of these [change] efforts accomplish their goals. Fewer than 15 of the 100 or more companies I have studied have successfully transformed themselves" (1998, p. 27). One problem, he says, is that leaders think change is about "writing a memo," or simply telling the organization to change. "Too often leaders launch their initiatives by calling a meeting or circulating a consultant's report, then expect people to rally to the cause. It doesn't happen that way."

Eric Charoux, executive director of DCDM Business School in Mauritius, found a better way. He realized he faced a choice in dealing with resistance to his plans for the school. "In setting up our governance policies and structures," he told me, "we began to encounter many obstacles, both from a resources and a psychological point of view. In handling these obstacles, we had two options: either the use of a top-down, forceful approach geared to overcoming them and implementing the required change—or the use of questions." He says that he and his colleagues realized that the use of questions would be the wiser choice:

> We began therefore to practice the discipline of asking questions as and when needed. We have found that asking questions generates further explorations, dispels confusion, brings about clarity, transforms conflict into confusion, empowers others, and changes frustration into satisfaction. Above all, questions generate commitment.

The extent to which change is embraced within an organization depends on how adept the leader is at engaging the staff in designing the organization's response to change. Effective leaders use questions to both motivate and guide the change effort. A question calls for an answer, so it acts as a catalyst to fresh thinking and helps to initiate new action (Blohowiak, 2000). By exploring some of the opportunities posed by strategically asked questions, staff can find new paths to explore for themselves and continue the development of their own careers. Effective leaders pose strategic questions and challenge their people to pursue the answers. Goldberg (1998a) notes how questions cause new openings whereas statements and opinions rarely do. Statements tend to lead to rote action. Effective questions, on the other hand, lead to effective action; ineffective or neglected questions result in detours, missed goals, and costly mistakes.

Rosabeth Moss Kanter says that change efforts require leaders to use questions to challenge the prevailing organizational wisdom:

Leaders need to develop what I call kaleidoscope thinking—a way of constructing patterns from the fragments of data available, and then manipulating them to form different patterns. They must question their assumptions about how pieces of the organization, the marketplace, or the community fit together. Change leaders remember that there are many solutions to a problem and that by looking through a different lens somebody is going to invent, for instance, a new way to deliver health care [1999, p. 17].

When leaders use questions to promote change, they demonstrate that they do not have all the answers and that they are willing to change themselves. This sends a powerful signal. Consider Cindy Stewart's experience:

When I became the CEO of the Family Health Council of Central Pennsylvania, Inc. in 1999, I needed to shift the culture from a task oriented hierarchy to a functional, empowered team environment. By leading through questions, I was able to act as a role model and demonstrate my willingness to learn, my desire to serve, and that humility can be inspiring. My employees have come to understand that I am a consultative leader and that it is critical to our success that they are knowledgeable of their customer expectations, willingly bring key information to the work process, and seek opportunity for continuous quality improvement.

When leading change, *how* questions are often the most powerful. We know where we want to go and the issue is *how to get there*. Frances Hesselbein of the Leader to Leader Institute suggests that leaders focus on *how* questions such as these: "How can we challenge the status quo—doing things *The Way*? How do we meet greater needs with diminishing resources? How do we bridge the divide between the field and the national organization?" She adds, "In these turbulent times, the questions we ask are almost more significant than the responses" (2003, p. 5). *How* questions empower others to find the way.

Gidget Hopf also uses *how* questions to shape a strategic vision at the Association for the Blind and Visually Impaired—Goodwill Industries in Rochester, New York. Some of the questions she used recently included

- How can we assure a prominent role for our mission in our quest for financial sustainability?

- How can the board hold staff accountable while not micromanaging?

- How can we more effectively communicate with the board about the difficult environment in which we try to develop new business?

Organizations that create learning environments make change a part of organizational life: after all, learning means changing. And as leaders, we can create agile, change-friendly organizations by asking questions and by encouraging a questioning culture throughout the organization.

Questions Transform Organizations

Questions have the power to transform organizations large and small. They can connect us to customers, markets, vendors, the community, and other stakeholders as we shape strategy. *How* questions can shape organizational values and bring commitment to them, and agile companies use questions to promote change.

"As we question and listen," Douglas Eden told me, "we develop credibility with the customers and build solid business relations. If we ask good questions and really listen, the solutions we select really work. We need to be humble, admitting we do not know all the answers, and thus we ask questions."

CONCLUSION

Becoming a Questioning Leader

Almost everyone has heard the adage, *You become what you think about*. What perhaps is even more true is that *we become what we ask about*. The people who are most successful in life do not get to the top because of what happens to them or what statements they make to others; they get to the top because of how they question what happens to them and the people and environment around them.

John Kotter, perhaps one of the most quoted experts on the subject of leadership, writes that the primary difference between leaders and managers is that leaders are those who ask the right questions whereas managers are those tasked to answer those questions (2002). Asking the right questions enables leaders to discover what is the right thing to do; answering them allows managers to do the right thing.

The importance and power of leading with questions is the theme of this book. Knowing when, where, why, and how to ask questions can help leaders strengthen relationships with staff, build powerful teams, create a strong learning culture, build relationships with customers and other stakeholders, and support strategic change. More than that, when we make asking questions a standard practice, it changes us.

Asking Questions Changes Us

Earlier chapters have emphasized the power of questions on those around the leader. However, questions have an impact on the leader as well. Questions help the questioners find a better understanding of themselves, comprehend more clearly why they do the things they do, and clarify their thinking. To operate in the world from the powerful position of a continuously developing learner, as Adams (2004) notes, one must develop a questing mindset. As Alcoa's Michael Coleman says, "My questions obviously impact me as leader. I see [asking questions] as the key way to gain knowledge. It has given me more confidence."

Kouzes and Posner (2003) explain how questions help us escape the trap of our own paradigms by broadening our perspectives and helping us to take responsibility for our own viewpoints. Zuboff (1989) remarks how we are "prisoners of our organizational vocabulary." Words can either trap us into a particular way of thinking about our roles and relationships or free us for wonderful new opportunities.

Questioning leaders are able to let go of their ego-driven need to have their own answers. They drop their need to be right, and so they can allow others to be right. They drop their protective barriers and are more open and vulnerable. Leaders who lead with questions are more easily able to drop their masks and facades and just be who they really are. Questions and answers work for those who are confident and flexible enough to make them work.

Questions help us redirect our mindset toward helping the other person achieve. This goes beyond the traditional notion of looking for growth opportunities in other people. Leaders who lead with questions recognize that they do not have all the answers. The resulting humility can be very powerful in being of service to others. Questions help us see that we can lead more effectively by serving than by directing. When you ask questions you show that you are committed to providing others the opportunity to lead you.

Becoming a Leader Who Asks Questions

When you move abruptly from being a leader who makes statements to one who asks questions, it may appear disconcerting, at least initially, to your colleagues—particularly subordinates. How then can a leader practice inquiry leadership and become more comfortable and better at asking questions? Marilee Adams (as cited in Blohowiak, 2000) suggests the following steps:

1. Start by becoming more aware of the questions you ask now and of the questions other people ask of you. Notice what works. We tend to answer reflectively, not thoughtfully, but effective questioning happens with conscious effort.

2. Try this simple experiment. Pick an hour and force yourself not to ask questions. This will focus your attention on the importance of questions. We tend to find ourselves asking questions mentally even if we are not voicing them.

3. Ask yourself more questions silently. Think about your thinking. As you become a conscious observer of your own thinking, you can shape it more intentionally, which will lead you to construct better, more effective questions that will lead to better answers and actions. For example, consciously ask yourself questions such as: What does this mean? Do I agree or disagree? How could this be helpful? How does this situation fit, contradict, or extend what I already believe to be true?

4. Before asking someone else a question, ask yourself this question: What do I want my question to accomplish? Intentionally frame your question so that you encourage collaborative thinking and cannot be perceived as threatening.

5. Encourage staff to ask you questions. This will, of course, lead to better thinking and actions.

Leading in the Twenty-First Century with Questions

John F. Kennedy, at his inaugural address in 1961, asked Americans to ask a different kind of question when he spoke these words: "Ask not what your country can do for you—ask what you can do for your country." Questions have an amazing degree of power, and

Kennedy's exhortation to Americans on that cold January morning in Washington, D.C.—to ask what they could do for their country— inspired an entire generation to reconsider their values and priorities, to serve others more than be served. Questions can indeed be that powerful. They are surely the most powerful tool that leaders can possibly employ, for they can accomplish enormous results; questions have the potency and force to change individuals, groups, organizations, communities, and even nations and the world.

The effective leaders of the future will need to consistently ask questions to receive feedback and to solicit new ideas. They will ask a variety of stakeholders for ideas, opinions, and feedback. Questions will be seen as a vital source of information for potential customers, suppliers, team members, cross-divisional people, direct reports, managers, other members of the organization, researchers, and thought leaders. The leaders will ask in a variety of ways: through leadership inventories, satisfaction surveys, phone calls, voice mail, e-mail, the Internet, satellite hookups, and in-person dialogue.

Leaders of the future will be more comfortable asking questions of their followers. They will encourage thought and guide with questions rather than answers. They will be open and honest, avoiding the appearance of being know-it-alls. Leaders of the future will be far more skilled at the art of questions than at the art of answering. Practicing this art demands levels of honesty and empowerment that are unknown in many of today's leaders. It is through this art that leaders can begin to share the burden of leadership with their followers, thereby increasing the capacity and performance of the organization.

Leaders who can ask, process information, and learn in a highly efficient manner will build organizations that have a tremendous competitive advantage over their slower and less proactive competition. Leaders who lead with questions will create a more humane workplace as well as a more successful business. Leaders who use questions can truly empower people and change organizations. My hope is that readers of this book will transform their style of leading from one of statements to one of questions, and thereby become successful and fulfilled as leaders in the twenty-first century.

Resource A

TRAINING PROGRAMS FOR QUESTIONING LEADERS

When in an epoch of change, when tomorrow is necessarily different from yesterday, new ways of thinking must emerge. New questions need to be asked before solutions are sought. [Leaders need] . . . to learn how to ask appropriate questions under conditions of risk rather than find answers to questions that have already been defined by others. We have to act ourselves into a new way of thinking rather than think ourselves into a new way of acting.

—*Reg Revans, father of action learning*

Two powerful programs are entering the leadership landscape whose primary focus is the development of leaders who lead with questions: *action learning* and *inquiry leadership training*. This resource describes each of these leadership programs and shows how and why they build questioning leaders.

How Action Learning Develops Questioning Leaders

More and more organizations around the world are using action learning as the primary method for developing their present and future leaders. Novartis, Nokia, Samsung, GE, Siemens, Boeing, and Constellation Energy are just a few of the companies that have made action learning the centerpiece of their leadership development programs. Academic institutions such as American University and Salford University have made action learning the cornerstone of their executive leadership programs.

What Is Action Learning?

Briefly defined, action learning is a process that involves people in a small group working on real problems and taking action, so that they learn as individuals, as a team, and as an organization while doing so (Marquardt, 1998, 2004). Action learning has six components:

1.   *A problem.* Action learning centers around a problem—a project, challenge, issue, or task, the resolution of which is of high importance to an individual, team, and/or organization. The problem should be significant and urgent, and should be the responsibility of the team to solve. It should also provide an opportunity for the group to generate learning opportunities, to build knowledge, and to develop individual, team, and organizational skills.

2.   *An action learning group.* The core entity in action learning is the action learning group (also called a *set* or *team*). The group is ideally composed of four to eight individuals who examine an organizational problem that has no easily identifiable solution. The group should have diversity of background and experience so as to acquire various perspectives and to encourage fresh viewpoints.

3.   *A process that emphasizes insightful questioning and reflective listening.* Action learning emphasizes questions and reflection above statements and opinions. By focusing on the right questions rather than the right answers, action learning brings out what one does not know as well as what one does know. Participants ask questions to clarify the exact nature of the problem, reflect and identify possible solutions, and only then take action. The focus is on questions because great solutions are contained within the seeds of great questions. Questions are used to build group dialogue and cohesiveness, generate innovative and systems thinking, and enhance learning results.

4.   *A requirement for action.* Action learning requires that the group be able to take action on the problem it is working on.

Members of the action learning group must have the power to take action themselves or be assured that their recommendations will be implemented, barring any significant change in the environment or the group's obvious lack of essential information. Action enhances learning because it provides a basis and anchor for the critical dimension of reflection. The *action* of action learning begins with taking steps to reframe the problem and determine the goal, and only then determining strategies and taking action.

5.   *A commitment to learning.* Solving an organizational problem provides immediate, short-term benefits to the company. The greater longer-term multiplier benefit, however, is the learning gained by each group member as well as by the group as a whole, and how those insights are applied on a system-wide basis throughout the organization. Thus the learning that occurs in action learning has greater value strategically for the organization than the immediate tactical advantage of early problem correction. Accordingly, action learning places equal emphasis on the learning and development of leaders and the team as it does on the solving of problems; the smarter the group becomes, the quicker and better will be the quality of its decision making and the action it takes.

6.   *An action learning coach.* Coaching is necessary for the group to focus on the important (that is, the learning) as well as the urgent (resolving the problem). The action learning coach helps the team members reflect both on what they are learning and on how they are solving problems. Through a series of questions, the coach enables group members to reflect on how they listen, how they may have reframed the problem, how they give each other feedback, how they are planning and working, and what assumptions may be shaping their beliefs and actions. The learning coach also helps the team focus on what they are achieving, what they are finding difficult, and on what processes they are employing and the implications of these processes. The coaching role may be rotated among members of the group or assigned to one person who holds that role throughout the duration of the group's existence.

How Does an Action Learning Program Work?

Action learning groups may meet once or several times, depending upon the complexity of the problem and the time available for its resolution. The action learning session may take place for one entire day, for a few hours over a few days, or over several months. A group may handle one or many problems. Whatever the time frame, however, action learning generally operates along the following stages and procedures:

1. *Formation of group:* The group may be volunteer or be appointed, and may be working on a single organizational problem or each other's departmental problems. The group may have a predetermined amount of time and sessions or it may determine the time parameters at the first meeting.

2. *Presentation of problem or task to group:* The problem is briefly presented to the group by the problem presenter, who may remain as a member of the group or withdraw and await the group's recommendations.

3. *Reframing the problem:* After a series of questions, the group, often with the guidance of the action learning coach, will reach a consensus as to the most critical and important problem that the group should work on and establish the crux of the problem, which may differ from the original presenting problem.

4. *Determining goals:* Once the key problem or issue has been identified, the group, again through the use of questions, seeks consensus for the goal whose achievement would solve the reframed problem for the long term with positive rather than negative consequences for the individual, team, or organization.

5. *Developing action strategies:* Much of the time and energy of the group will be spent on identifying and pilot-testing possible action strategies. Like the preceding stages of action learning, strategies are developed via questions and reflective dialogue.

6. *Taking action:* Between action learning sessions, the group as a whole as well as individual members collect information, identify status of support, and implement the strategies developed and agreed to by the group.

7. *Capturing learnings:* Throughout and at any point during the sessions, the action learning coach may intervene to ask the group members questions that will enable them to clarify the problem, find ways to improve their performance as a group, and identify how their learnings can be applied to develop the members themselves, the team, and the organization.

How Action Learning Develops Inquiry Leadership

Dilworth (1998) notes that leadership development programs, as practiced by most organizations, "produce individuals who are technologically literate and able to deal with intricate problem-solving models, but are essentially distanced from the human dimensions that must be taken into account. Leaders thus may become good at downsizing and corporate restructuring, but cannot deal with a demoralized workforce and the resulting longer-term challenges" (p. 49). Action learning differs from normal leadership development programs in that it requires the individuals and group members to ask appropriate questions in conditions of risk, rather than to find answers that have already been precisely defined by others (Revans, 1982).

Most management development programs focus on a single dimension. By contrast, action learning derives its power from the fact that it does not isolate any dimension from the context in which the managers work. Instead, it develops the whole leader for the whole organization. What leaders learn and how they learn cannot be dissociated from one another, for *how* one learns necessarily influences *what* one learns. The *how* of action learning is through the mode of questioning.

Learning cannot be solely the acquisition of existing knowledge. Managers need also to improve their ability to search the unfamiliar. Dilworth (1998) notes that action learning provides leadership skills that encourage fresh thinking, and thus it enables leaders to avoid responding to today's problems with yesterday's solutions while tomorrow's challenges engulf them. Action learning provides managers the opportunity to take "appropriate levels of responsibility in discovering how to develop themselves" (p. 37).

Mumford (1995) believes action learning is so effective in developing leaders because it incorporates three crucial elements in management development: (1) taking action leads to more learning than can be derived from merely diagnosing and analyzing or recommending action, as most leadership development programs do; (2) working on projects that are significant and meaningful to the managers themselves creates greater learning for them than they'd get from going through the motions on abstract problems; (3) leaders learn better from one another than from instructors who are not managers or who have never managed.

A key outcome of action learning is the development of leaders who incorporate questioning as an integral way of leading. In action learning, everyone receives ample time to practice and demonstrate the art of asking questions. Questions are at the heart of action learning and contribute immensely to its success. With the guidance of the action learning coach, the group reflects on the quality and impact of each individual's questions as well as those of the group. In action learning, finding the right question is more important than answering the wrong question, no matter how well it is answered. This habit of questioning others as well as oneself represents a unique strength of action learning (McNulty & Canty, 1994).

As noted, the primary ways in which action learning differs from other leadership programs and problem-solving approaches is its focus on questions rather than on solutions. Only through questions can a group truly gain a common understanding of the problem, acquire a sense of each member's potential strategies, and achieve innovative breakthrough strategies and solutions. Questions, when asked at the right time in the right way, provide the glue that brings and holds the group together. The seeds of the answer are contained in the questions. Thus the better the questions, the better the solutions—and the learning; the deeper the reflection, the greater the development of individual and team competencies.

Questions serve many purposes for action learning groups. They enable members to understand, to clarify, and to open up new avenues of exploration for solving the problem. They provide new insights and ideas for strategic actions and potential paths for solutions. Questions build understanding while laying the groundwork for gaining support for possible action. Questions also serve as the foundation for individual, team, and organizational learning, and especially the development of inquiring leaders.

Statements Only in Response to Questions

Much of the potency of action learning is built upon questions that generate reflective inquiry. Therefore, it is highly encouraged that action learning groups and the action learning coach establish this ground rule during their sessions: *Statements can only be made in response to a question.*

This ground rule does not prohibit the use of statements; as a matter of fact, there may still be more statements than questions during the action learning meetings since every question asked may generate one or more responses from each of the other members of the group, or as many as five or ten statements per question.

However, by requiring people to think "questions first," the entire dynamics of the group is transformed. The natural impulse to make statements and judgments changes to one of listening and reflecting. Once the problem or task has been introduced to the group, the members must first ask questions to clarify the problem before jumping into statements solving the problem. In action learning, we recognize that there is almost a direct correlation between the number and quality of questions and the eventual quality of the final actions and learnings. Balancing the number of questions and the number of statements leads to dialogue, which is a proper balance between advocating and inquiring.

This ground rule provides tremendous value to the action learning group. First, it forces everyone in the group to think about asking questions, about inquiring rather than making statements and advocating positions. Questions tend to unite; statements can cause divisions. An environment in which questions are valued requires people to listen to each other. Questions prevent domination by a single person and instead create cohesion.

Two questions are often raised about this ground rule. First, doesn't this ground rule limit the free flow of interaction among group members? Yes, it may slow down the rapid flow of communication, but in action learning this is seen as a positive as it forces members to be more reflective and creative, to listen first. Second, won't some people be able to manipulate this rule, and merely raise their voice at the end of a statement and thereby convert it into a question? This is certainly possible, but once any statement is converted into a question, the power then moves to the respondents who may choose to agree or not agree, may choose to reflect upon the question, or may respond with a more open question of their own.

Action learning members quickly become comfortable and competent in this approach to communications. As action learning groups experience the tremendous benefits of questioning, they gladly embrace this precept. It recaptures their natural way of communicating and learning—the one they used as toddlers, before it got stamped out by the adults who kept saying, "Stop asking so many questions!" The quality of the group's work and the comfort of the interactions oftentimes cause members to apply this ground rule in other parts of organizational life.

In most problem-solving situations, only the knowledge that is brought into the group by its members is considered and applied. This limited knowledge allows only for an incremental, narrowly focused understanding and mediocre solution to the problem; it rarely generates the quantum improvements or spectacular leaps in knowledge necessary to solve today's more complex problems. Programmed knowledge alone is simply unable to solve problems from a systems perspective.

Only through questions and reflections (that is, the reflective inquiry process of action learning) can a group generate a holistic, broad-based perspective. By seeing each other as learners and learning resources, members of action learning group anticipate the generation of new knowledge within the group. Questioning builds on the knowledge that people bring into the group while at the same time constructing new knowledge and learning.

By beginning with questioning rather than using past knowledge as the first reference point, the group can gauge whether the information presently available is adequate and relevant to the situation. The key to problem solving is to start with fresh questions, not constructs and assumptions from the past. Questions enable groups to unpeel the layers around the problem and uncover the core elements of knowledge necessary to discover the solution.

The Leader as an Action Learning Coach

The skills and practice of leading with questions can be developed in action learning in the group member role, but they develop even more powerfully when the leader takes a turn as coach. A number of important questioning skills, values, and attributes are developed in serving as an action learning coach:

• *Ability to ask questions.* The key skill of the action learning coach is the ability to ask good questions, both initial and especially follow-up questions. The coach needs to be able to ask questions that make people think and feel challenged; the questions should be supportive and positive rather than critical. To consistently ask good questions, the action learning coach needs a strong and sincere belief in the power of questions and the critical role of action learning coach in asking questions. The manner of introducing questions should be gentle and not arrogant, so the coach needs to look inward and determine whether a chosen question will be truly helpful to the group, one with the potential to create possibilities for significant learning and breakthrough action.

• *Courage and authenticity.* Asking questions is not always easy, especially the tough follow-up questions or questions that require deep and intensive soul-searching. The action learning coach needs to be courageous and authentic, strong and unintimidated by the rank or expertise or character of the person to whom the question is posed, and willing to pursue doubts about the existence of agreement or clarity.

• *A sense of timing.* Finding the ideal time for intervening is an art for the action learning coach. Intervene too early, and the group or individual may not have enough experience to have developed sufficient data to respond adequately, and thus may miss an opportunity for understanding. Intervene too late, and the group's overlong struggle may lead to frustration and a missed opportunity for learning. Experience will make the coach grow more comfortable and confident in intervention timing. And, though timing is important, any time that one intervenes can be an occasion of great learning.

• *Confidence and trust in the process and the people in the group.* The action learning coach must be confident in the role and must demonstrate this confidence by displaying a relaxed belief in the action learning process and the eventual success of the group. The coach should radiate assurance that the action learning process will work, that the theories and principles underlying it (namely, the six components and two rules) are demonstrably sound. The coach should believe that everyone in the group has abilities necessary to solve the problem, so the coach's job is merely to bring out and capitalize on these strengths: to get the group from today to tomorrow. (This is unlike the job of a therapist, who seeks to get you from yesterday to today.) With a strong confidence in the success of the process and the people, the action learning coach is able to tolerate ambiguity more easily.

- *Values and characteristics.* The action learning coach, because of the power inherent in the role, should be cognizant of the way personal values and actions affect the group and the action learning process. By presence alone, the coach has a significant impact on the group; the members know that the coach may raise questions at any point that will challenge their thinking and actions, decisions made and not made. Therefore, a number of characteristics are fitting for an action learning coach, including openness, patience, honesty and integrity, humility, the ability to be nonjudgmental, and the capacity for reflection. Like the leader in Herman Hesse's *Journey to the East,* the action learning coach is so subtle and natural that the group does not realize how powerful and beneficial the coach's influence is. They do not realize its value unless or until they no longer have the coach to rely upon.

- *Strong coordination and planning skills.* As noted earlier in this chapter, the action learning coach has a variety of other roles in addition to serving as a coach to an action learning group. These other roles require strong coordination skills, the ability see the big picture and not become lost in details. Since the coach needs to be able to maintain working and supportive relationships with so many people inside and outside the group and even the organization, the role requires the ability to keep many balls in the air at the same time.

- *Good listening skills.* Successful action learning coaches need to possess strong listening skills. They should be able to hear what is not said as well as what is said. Careful observation and good note taking allow them to be in tune with who is saying what, how, when, and to whom. Active listening requires a great deal of attention. This strong listening enables them to acquire a "helicopter-type" perspective and holistic view. They must be able to stand apart from the problem and focus on the development of the group.

- *Strong commitment to learning.* Action learning coaches must be eager to see people learn. As tempting as it may be to do otherwise during the action learning sessions, they focus on the learning, not on the issue or problem being discussed. They understand and appreciate how adults learn and they see learning as a way of life. And they recognize that learners can only learn for themselves (Boud et al., 1985).

• *Attitude toward group members.* Effective action learning coaches respect each person and have concern for the well-being of all members. They want everyone to succeed with the project and to learn from so doing. This ability to empathize and be supportive is very important. They should see members as curious and thoughtful about the problem and about each other. These attitudes generate more trust toward the coach as well as more openness among the group members.

• *Self-awareness and self-confidence.* Action learning coaches need to be cognizant of their own strengths and limitations, with enough self-confidence to be authentic and resilient. Their humility allows them to demonstrate themselves as still willing and able to learn. They should want to be seen as people who can be trusted, who can handle rivalries, distrust, and anger.

For more information about action learning, see the Web site of the Global Institute for Action Learning: http://www.managementconcepts.com/gial/gial.asp.

The Institute for Inquiring Leadership

A second resource that is gaining increasing popularity in developing questioning leaders is the Institute for Inquiring Leadership (IIL), which has a number of training programs designed to promote the expert application of inquiry and reflection skills by leaders and managers to themselves, others, and their organizations (Adams, 2004). The training programs seek to develop eight characteristics that IIL research shows to be important for inquiring leaders:

• An insatiable, nonjudgmental curiosity that places a high value on continuous learning for themselves and others and allows them to model inquiry that is constructive rather than criticizing.

- A commitment to establishing an inquiring culture (both formal and informal) in their organizations and teams, appreciating that many people have some reluctance about asking questions and need to be encouraged to do so.

- An ability to challenge assumptions and beliefs in thinking and communication, solicit honest feedback, and suspend their own opinions in the face of new data, and to "not know" and "not be right."

- An ability to listen carefully and thoroughly, especially when not liking or agreeing with what they may be hearing. This includes questioning people about their opinions, perspectives, motivations, needs, and expectations.

- A commitment to take *reflecting time* when formulating questions and answers and encourage others to do the same.

- A commitment to institute standard, inquiry-based problem-solving and learning practices, especially those based on principles of action learning.

- An ability to intentionally ask themselves and others questions that open thinking, to challenge assumptions, and to seek creative solutions, as well as to think about their own thinking (and question their questions) and to manage their thinking, feeling, and behaviors.

- The strength to be decisive and committed to strategic rather than reactive action.

QuestionThinking™ (QT), the system of techniques at the heart of IIL's training programs for developing the inquiring leader, is based upon the following core premises:

- Thinking occurs as an internal question-and-answer process, regardless of whether the individual is aware of this. In other words, thoughts that are statements represent answers to preceding thoughts that are questions.

- These internal questions virtually program thoughts, feelings, behaviors, and outcomes, whether or not an individual is aware of having asked those questions.

- Internal questions are the key points for understanding mental models, uncovering assumptions, altering attitudes and patterns of interaction, and creating different results.

- Therefore, it is important to learn how to discern the questions being asked, employ models for analyzing these questions for effectiveness, and develop skills to revise the questions if better ones could lead to better results.

- Effective questions (either internal or interpersonal questions) lead to effective results, ineffective questions to ineffective results, missed or avoided questions to unpredictable (and sometimes problematic) results.

- Most people are barely aware of the existence, prevalence, relevance, or power of internal (or interpersonal) questions and therefore lack both the motivation and ability to take advantage of this naturally occurring cognitive and linguistic resource.

IIL considers coaching a core competence for inquiring leaders and most of its training programs are designed around this premise. Whether focused on developing future leaders, providing performance feedback, or leading a productive team or project, coaching is a vital set of skills for leaders at all levels of an organization.

The Institute for Inquiring Leadership flagship program is "The Inquiring Leader: Coaching for Results." This two-day interactive training program for leaders at all levels is designed to develop leadership, coaching, and questioning skills. The course is based on QuestionThinking methods and tools as well as many of the central premises of action learning. These are the goals, in more detail:

- Reinforcing a leadership mindset based on curiosity and questions, moving away from a leadership mindset based on opinions and statements.

- Developing a commitment to use coaching attitudes and skills as a core competence of leadership.

- Learning the attitudes and skill sets of coaching in a way that is practical, simple to use, compelling, self-reinforcing, and self-generating.

- Producing the kind of breakthrough in thinking (in the course) that can lead to a breakthrough in results (after the course) for each participant in relation to the real-time business challenge each selects to focus on in the program.

- Integrating these methods and tools along with the ability to apply them consistently and successfully after the course in leadership situations other than coaching.

The theme of the first day of the "Inquiring Leader: Coaching for Results" workshop is to provide the background theory and fundamental leadership mindset and practices required for successful coaching. Participants learn how QuestionThinking and question asking are the core competences of coaching and are introduced to practical methods for taking advantage of this understanding. Each selects a coaching learning partner with whom to work in coaching sessions throughout the two days. Each also selects an important real-time business challenge, issue, or project as the practical lens through which to learn QT and coaching fundamentals. This real-time challenge will be the focus of the coaching sessions with the learning partner throughout the workshop. One of the responsibilities of the learning partner will be to ask fresh questions that challenge prior conceptions of the "problem" that may be impeding new thinking and the possibility of novel solutions.

The theme of the second day of the course is "practice, practice, practice." First participants practice delivering empowering and accurate feedback in coaching conversations. Then they are introduced to the Question Map, a process that guides them through each of the stages of a coaching conversation, including the goals, QT tools and practices, and kinds of questions required to be most thorough and successful at each stage.

One of the primary QT practices that each individual partici-pant will experience is called Q-Storming. This exercise is like advanced brainstorming, but with an important difference. The goal is to generate as many new questions as possible, assuming that this is a most powerful path for discovering new directions, possi-bilities, and solutions. The exercise illustrates the maxim, "A ques-tion not asked is a door not opened"—and demonstrates that almost any problem can be solved with enough right questions. The participants each experience a Q-Storming session focused on their real-time business challenge so that each emerges from the course with new questions that can lead to new thinking, behaviors, and possibilities with respect to their business challenge.

For more information about the Institute for Inquiring Leader-ship, see the Web site: http://www.inquiryinc.com/.

Resource B

BIOGRAPHIES OF LEADERS INTERVIEWED

Frank Andracchi is vice president of Constellation Generation Group. He has been in the power industry since 1969, as an engineer, construction supervisor, division manager, plant manager, and regional manager. Prior to joining Constellation, Frank was a regional manager for resource recovery operations for Ogden Allied Services and spent nineteen years with Long Island Lighting Company.

Jeff Carew has worked at Collectcorp since January 1992, starting as a junior collector at $1200 per month. He is now vice president of collections. Collectcorp serves major credit grantors in the United States and Canada and has more than 650 employees.

Eric Charoux is a partner at De Chazal Du Mee and executive director of DCDM Business School in Mauritius. Eric has extensive experience assessing and developing executives, managers, and supervisors in Africa, having worked with large organizations in Botswana, South Africa, Swaziland, and Zimbabwe. He is the author of three books and more than fifty articles and research papers on topics such as organizational development, change management through action learning, assessing and developing leadership potential, and managerial interpersonal effectiveness.

Mike Coleman, vice president of the Alcoa Rigid Packaging business unit in Knoxville, Tennessee, is responsible for Alcoa's aluminum can recycling activities. He is a member of Alcoa's Executive Council, the senior leadership group that provides strategic direction for the company. Prior to joining Alcoa in 1998, Mike was president of North Star Steel. He serves on the Board of Directors of the Steel Manufacturers' Association and on the Executive Committee of the Association of Iron and Steel Engineers.

Doug Eden began his career with Cargill in 1978 as a staff accountant in Minneapolis. He served in senior management positions in Thailand and Australia as well as eight cities in the United States before becoming president of Malt Americas.

Mark Harper is currently president of wholesale marketing for ConocoPhillips Petroleum in the United States. He has more than twenty-four years of marketing experience, ranging from packaged goods to food service to petroleum marketing. His prior employers include British Petroleum, Tosco, and Phillips Petroleum.

Robert Hoffman is executive director for organization development at Novartis, where he has worked since 2001. Prior to joining Novartis, Bob spent twelve years with Warner-Lambert, serving in a variety of corporate human resources positions. He supported the U.S. Sales and Marketing organizations and was ultimately asked to join the "Go-To-Market" project on a full-time basis, helping Parke-Davis adopt key learnings from its successful launch of Lipitor, the world's largest-selling pharmaceutical product. When Warner-Lambert was acquired by Pfizer, Bob was one of four people chosen in Ann Arbor to provide full-time support to the integration activities. These activities were widely seen as best practice and were documented extensively in the press and academic literature.

Chad Holliday is chairman of the board and CEO of DuPont. Chad is the eighteenth executive to lead the company in the more than two hundred years of DuPont history. Chad is past chairman of the World Business Council for Sustainable Development (WBCSD) and has coauthored *Walking the Talk,* a book that details the business case for sustainable development and corporate responsibility.

Gidget Hopf, president and CEO of the Association for the Blind and Visually Impaired—Goodwill Industries in Rochester, New York, has spent her entire career in the field of disabilities, first with people who are developmentally disabled and, since 1986, with people who are blind. The Rochester program provides comprehensive rehabilitation, career, and training services. It has a food services business as well as a manufacturing division employing eighty people who are blind or visually impaired. Gidget has a doctoral degree in human resource development from George Washington University.

Tom Laughlin is president of Caravela Inc., an international leadership and team development consulting firm based in Minneapolis, Minnesota. He has served as marketing director in the Baking Products Division at General Mills and has also held management positions in sales, production, and general operations in a number of start-up companies.

Rick Lendemann is the associate dean of Facilities College, Sodexho University, where he manages an action learning accredited degree program. He is a graduate of Brigham Young University in Provo, Utah, with a bachelor of science degree in Latin American Studies.

Suzanne Milchling is head of the Homeland Defense Business Unit, Department of Defense, whose mission is to enhance the response capabilities of military, federal, state, and local emergency responders to terrorist incidents involving weapons of mass destruction.

Kook-Hyun Moon, president and CEO of Yuhan-Kimberly, is well known for his leading by questions. During his twenty-nine years at the company, Moon has used various methods of questioning. Yuhan-Kimberly is a joint-venture consumer product company between Kimberly-Clark Corporation of USA and Yuhan Corporation of Korea. Yuhan-Kimberly is known as one of the most admired companies in Korea and has won the "Best Employer in Asia Award" in the 2003 surveys implemented by Hewitt Associates.

Charles Ostland recently retired after twenty-five years' experience as a teacher before becoming principal of Oakton High School in 1999 where he managed a staff of 220, including nearly 160 teachers. The staff is a great mixture of veteran educators and newcomers, all of whom, as he notes, "dedicate themselves to the success of the school." Oakton High School is a school of approximately twenty-three hundred students with approximately 25 percent minority population.

Jeanette Partlow is president of Maryland Chemical Company, Inc. Customers' markets include food and beverage; environmental protection and remediation; metal working; chemical, pharmaceuticals, and electronics manufacturing; and other general industrial applications. She is currently leading a culture transition to a performance management system and a new generation of owner-managers.

Effendy Mohamed Rajab is the senior training and development director for the World Organization of the Scout Movement, headquartered in Geneva, Switzerland. There are currently 154 National Scout Organizations in the world. Effendy worked as a senior fire and security officer in a petrochemical complex for nineteen years before becoming executive director of Singapore Scouts Association in 2000.

Isabel Rimanoczy is a partner with LIM (Leadership in International Management) and has authored numerous articles based on her work in Latin America, Europe, the United States, and Asia. She trained more than 150 learning coaches and coauthored the *Learning Coach Handbook*, the *Leader Coach Handbook*, and the *Mergers and Acquisitions Integration Handbook*. She is the editor of a monthly electronic newsletter on leadership topics. Isabel is a doctoral candidate at Columbia University and an executive coach, using action reflection learning to develop high-performing teams and leaders.

David Smyk has more than twenty years' experience in corporate treasury, financial reporting, accounts receivable collections, credit extension, and human resource management with firms such as Aetna Healthcare, Philips, Polaroid, and Sharp Electronics. In 2001, he became a partner in a sales and strategic thinking firm known as Healthcare Executive Partners.

Cindy Stewart is president and CEO of the Family Health Council of Central Pennsylvania. Previously she was president and CEO of Family Service of Lancaster County and executive director of the Welsh Mountain Medical and Dental Center, a community health center located in rural Lancaster County. Cindy currently serves as Chairman of the Lancaster County Housing & Redevelopment Authority, and as President of the Pennsylvania Society of Association Executives. She has served as chairman of the board of the Family Health Council of Central Pennsylvania and president of the Pennsylvania Council of Family Agencies.

Pentti Sydanmaanlakka has a wide range of experience in all areas of human resource management in Europe, the United States, and Asia. From 1993, he worked as a director of human resources in Nokia Networks. In 2002 he started his own consultancy, Pertec Consulting. He has also been chairman of the Finnish Association of Human Resource Management and has worked for Nixdorf Computer, Siemens Nixdorf Information Systems, Kone Corporation, and VIA Group. He is the author of *An Intelligent Organization*.

Mark Thornhill became CEO of the Midwest Region of the American Red Cross in January 2002. Prior to this, Mark served as chief administrative officer and director of donor services of the New York-Penn Region, where he led that region in its successful 28 percent increase in whole blood collections, and nearly 300 percent increase in AB plasma collection. Under his leadership, the associated costs of collecting blood decreased by 27 percent, and the processing time per unit decreased by 15 percent. Prior to leading New York-Penn Region, Mark served as director of donor resources and director of manufacturing and distribution in the Alabama Region in Birmingham.

Sue Whitt has more than twenty-five years of corporate leadership experience and consulting expertise. She has held a wide variety of senior leadership roles in the pharmaceutical industry including positions at Warner Lambert Parke-Davis, Pfizer and Abbott Labs. Sue has managed information technology groups as well as accountants, having begun her career as a C.P.A. She consulted for several years for public and nonprofit organizations in the areas of leadership development and organizational readiness.

Bibliography

Abrahamson, M. (1997). New behaviors, new roles and new attitudes. *Public Manager, 26*(1), 1–5.

Abrashoff, D. M. (2002). *It's your ship: Management techniques from the best damn ship in the Navy.* New York: Warner Books.

Adams, M. (2004). *Change your questions, change your life: 7 powerful tools for life and work.* San Francisco: Berrett-Koehler.

Adams, M., Schiller, M., & Cooperrider, D. (2004). With our questions we make our world." In D. Cooperrider & M. Avital, *Advances in appreciative inquiry. Vol. 1: Constructive discourse and human organization.* London: Elsevier.

Allee, V. (1997). *The knowledge evolution.* New York: Butterworth-Heinemann.

Austin, J. E. (1998, Spring). The invisible side of leadership. *Leader to Leader,* (8), 38–46.

Axelrod, R. H., Axelrod, E. M., Beedon, J., & Jacobs, R. W. (2005, Spring). Creating dynamic, energy-producing meetings. *Leader to Leader,* (36), 53–58.

Badaracco, J. (2002). *Leading quietly.* Boston: Harvard Business School Press.

Bandura, A. (1977). *Social learning theory.* Upper Saddle River, NJ: Prentice-Hall.

Bass, B. (1985). *Leadership and performance beyond expectations.* New York: Free Press.

Bell, C., & Bell, B. (2003). *Magnetic service: Secrets of creating passionately devoted customers.* San Francisco: Berrett-Koehler.

Bennis, W., & Thomas, R. (2002). *Geeks and geezers: How eras, values and defining moments shape leaders.* Boston: Harvard Business School Press.

Bianco-Mathis, V., Nabors, L., & Roman, C. (2002). *Leading from the inside out.* Thousand Oaks, CA: Sage.

Blanchard, K. (2003). *The servant leader.* Nashville, TN: Countryman.

Blanchard, K., & Stoner, J. (2003). *Full steam ahead.* San Francisco: Berrett-Koehler.

Block, P. (1999). *Flawless consulting.* San Francisco: Jossey-Bass.

Block, P. (2003, May). "Strategies of Consent." Handout at 2003 ASTD Conference, Atlanta.

Blohowiak, D. (2000). Question your way to the top! *Productive Leader, 121,* 1–3.

Bollier, D. (1996). *Aiming higher*. New York: AMACOM.

Bossidy, L., & Charan, R. (2002). *Execution: The discipline of getting things done*. New York: Crown.

Boud, D., Keogh, R., & Walker, D. (1985). *Reflection: Turning experience into learning*. London: Kogan Page.

Bowie, N. (2000). A Kantian theory of leadership. *Leadership & Organization Development Journal, 1*(4), 185–193.

Browne, M., & Keeley, S. (2001). *Asking the right questions: A guide to critical thinking* (6th ed.). Upper Saddle River, NJ: Prentice Hall.

Bruner, J. (1974). *Toward a theory in instruction*. Cambridge: Belknap Press.

Carkhuff, R. (1969). *Helping and human relations*. Amherst, MA: HRD Press.

Champy, J. (2000, Summer). The residue of leadership: Why ambition matters. *Leader to Leader*, (17), 14–19.

Clarke-Epstein, C. (2002). *Seventy-eight important questions every leader should ask and answer*. New York: AMACOM.

Clemens, J., & Mayer, D. (1987). *The classic touch: Lessons in leadership from Homer to Hemingway*. Homewood, IL: Irwin.

Cohen, E., & Tichy, N. (2002). *The leadership engine*. New York: HarperBusiness.

Cockman, P., Evans, B., & Reynolds, P. (1992). *Client-centered consulting*. New York: McGraw-Hill.

Coffman, V. (2002, August). Interview with Lockheed Martin Chairman and CEO Vance Coffman. *Academy of Management Executive, 16*(3), 31–40.

Collins, J. (2001). *Good to great*. New York: HarperBusiness.

Colvin, F. (2001). The anti-control freak. *Fortune, 144*(11), 60.

Cook, M., & Jackson, N. (2001, December 11). Weakest links in the supply chain. *Financial Times*. Available online: http: www.bain.com/bainweb/publications/publications_overview.asp. Access date: March 21, 2005.

Cooperrider, D. (Ed.). (2001). *Appreciative inquiry: An emerging direction for organization development*. Champaign, IL: Stipes Press.

Crowley, J. (2004). Enlightened leadership in the U.S. Navy. Available online: http://enlightenedleadershipsolutions.com/lmd/lmd_articles.html. Access date: March 21, 2005.

Daudelin, M. (1996). Learning from experience. *Organization Dynamics, 24*(3), 36-48.

Dillon, J. (1988). *Questioning and teaching*. New York: Teachers College Press.

Dilworth, L. (1998). Action learning in a nutshell. *Performance Improvement Quarterly, 11*(1), 28–43.

Duncan, E., & Warden, G. (1999). Influential leadership and change environment: The role leaders play in the growth and development of the people they lead. *Journal of Healthcare Management, 44*(4), 225–226.

Drucker, P. (2003). *The essential Drucker*. New York: HarperBusiness.

Drucker, P. F., & Maciariello, J. A. (2004). *The daily Drucker*. New York: HarperBusiness.

Finkelstein, S. (2003). *Why smart executives fail*. New York: Portfolio.

Finkelstein, S. (2004, Winter). Zombie businesses: How to learn from their mistakes. *Leader to Leader*, (32), 25–31.

Goldberg, M. (1998a). *The art of the question: A guide to short-term question-centered therapy*. New York: Wiley.

Goldberg, M. (1998b). The spirit and discipline of organizational inquiry. *Manchester Review*, (3), 1–7.

Goldberg, M. (1999). Expert question asking: The engine of successful coaching. *Manchester Review*, (4), 1–7.

Goldsmith, M. (1996). Ask, learn, follow up, and grow. In F. Hesselbein, M. Goldsmith, & R. Beckhard (Eds.), *The leader of the future: New visions, strategies, and practices for the next era*, 227–237. San Francisco: Jossey-Bass.

Goldsmith, M. (2000). *Coaching for leadership*. New York: Pfeiffer.

Hamel, G. (2003). A new way of seeing the world. *Executive Excellence*, 20(2), 16–17.

Hammer, M. (2001). *What every business must do to dominate the decade*. New York: Crown Business.

Hammer, M., & Stanton, S. (1997, November 24). The power of reflection. *Fortune*, 136(10), 291–294.

Harbison, J. R., & Pekar, P., Jr. (1998, second quarter). Institutionalizing alliance skills: Secrets of repeatable success. *strategy+business*. Available online with registration: http://www.strategy-business.com/press/article/15893?pg=0. Access date: March 21, 2005.

Heenan, D., & Bennis, W. (1999). *Co-leaders*. New York: Wiley.

Heifetz, R. (1994). *Leadership without easy answers*. Cambridge, MA: Harvard University Press.

Heifetz, R. & Laurie, D. (1997). The work of leadership. *Harvard Business Review*, 75(1), 124–134.

Heifetz, R., & Linsky, M. (2002). *Leadership on the line*. Boston: Harvard Business School Press.

Heimbold, C. (1999). Attributes and formation of good leaders. *Vital Speeches of the Day*, 65(6), 179–181.

Hesselbein, F. (2001, Spring). When the roll is called in 2010. *Leader to Leader*, (20), 4–6.

Hesselbein, F. (2003, Winter). Finding the right questions. *Leader to Leader*, (27), 4–6.

Hesselbein, F. (2005, Winter). The leaders we need. *Leader to Leader*, (35), 4–5.

Hesselbein, F., Goldsmith, M., & Beckhard, R. (1996). *The leader of the future: New visions, strategies, and practices for the next era*. San Francisco: Jossey-Bass.

Hii, A. (2000). *The impact of action learning on the conflict-handling styles of managers in a Malaysian firm*. Unpublished doctoral dissertation, George Washington University.

Hofstede, G. (1992). *Culture and organizations*. London: McGraw-Hill.

Hymowitz, C. (2004, December 28). Some tips from CEOs. *Wall Street Journal*, p. B1.

Isaacs, W. (1993, August). Taking flight: Dialogue, collective thinking and organizational learning. *Organizational Dynamics*, pp. 24–39.

Janis, I. L. (1971). Groupthink. *Psychology Today*, 5(6), 43–44, 46, 74–76.

Kanter, R. M. (1999, Summer). The enduring skills of change leaders. *Leader to Leader*, (13), 15–22.

Knowles, M., Holton, E., & Swanson, R. (1998). *The adult learner*. Houston: Gulf.

Knowling, R., Jr. (2002). Leading with vision, strategy, and values. In Frances Hesselbein, Marshall Goldsmith, & Iain Somerville (Eds.), *Leading for innovation*. San Francisco: Jossey-Bass.

Kotter, J. P. (1998, Fall). Winning at change. *Leader to Leader*, (10), 27–33.

Kotter, J. (2002). *The heart of change*. Cambridge, MA: Harvard Business School Press.

Kouzes, J., & Posner, B. (2002). *The leadership challenge* (3rd ed.). San Francisco: Jossey-Bass.

Leeds, D. (1987). *Smart questions: The essential strategy for successful managers*. New York: McGraw-Hill.

Leeds, D. (2000). *The seven powers of questions*. New York: Perigee Books.

Lencioni, P. M. (2003, Summer). The trouble with teamwork. *Leader to Leader*, (29), 35–40.

Levi, D. (2001). *Group dynamics for teams*. Thousand Oaks, CA: Sage.

Manville, B. (2001, Spring). Learning in the new economy. *Leader to Leader*, (20), 36–45.

Marquardt, M. (1998). *Action learning in action*. Palo Alto, CA: Davies-Black.

Marquardt, M. (2000). *The global advantage*. Houston: Gulf.

Marquardt, M. (2003). *Building the learning organization: Mastering the five elements for corporate learning*. Palo Alto, CA: Davies-Black.

Marquardt, M. (2004). *Optimizing the power of action learning*. Palo Alto, CA: Davies-Black.

Marquardt, M., & Berger, N. (2000). *Global leaders for the twenty-first century*. Albany: State University of New York Press.

Marquardt, M., Berger, N., & Loan, P. (2004). *HRD in the age of globalization*. New York: Basic Books.

Marsick, V. (1992). Experiential-based executive learning outside the classroom. *Journal of Management Development*, 46(8), 50–60.

Martin, J. (2002). Questioning for success. Exec online. Available online: http://www.unisys.com/execmag/strategy/internal/leadership/2002_12_dialog.htm. Access date: March 21, 2005.

McNulty, N., & Canty, G. (1995). Proof of the pudding. *Journal of Management Education*, 14(1), 53–66.

Mezirow, J. (1991). *Transformative dimensions of adult learning*. San Francisco: Jossey-Bass.

Mill, J. S. (1998). *On liberty and other essays*. Oxford: Oxford University Press. (Original work published 1859)

Mitroff, I. (1998). *Smart thinking for crazy times: The art of solving the right problems*. San Francisco: Berrett-Koehler.

Mittelstaedt, R. E. (2005). *Will your next mistake be fatal?* Upper Saddle River, NJ: Wharton School.

Mobley, S. (1999). Judge not: How coaches create healthy organizations. *Journal for Quality and Participation, 22*(4), 57–60.

Morris, J. (1991). Minding our Ps and Qs. In M. Pedler (Ed.), *Action learning in practice*. Aldershot, England: Gower.

Mumford, A. (1995). Developing others through action learning. *Industrial and Commercial Training, 27*(2), 19–27.

Nadler, G., & Chandon, W. (2004). *Smart questions: Learn to ask the right questions for powerful results*. San Francisco: Jossey-Bass.

Oakley, D., & Krug, D. (1991). *Enlightened leadership*. New York: Simon & Schuster.

Parker, M. (2001, December). Breakthrough leadership. *Harvard Business Review*, p. 37.

Peters, T. (1992). *Liberation management*. New York: Knopf.

Revans, R. (1982). *The origins and growth of action learning*. Bromley, England: Chartwell Brat.

Rilke, R. (1903). *Letters to a young poet*. New York: Norton.

Rogers, C. (1961). *On becoming a person*. Boston: Houghton Mifflin.

Rosen, R., & Paul, B. (1996). *Leading people: Transforming business from the inside out*. New York: Viking.

Schein, E. (2004). *Organizational culture and leadership*. San Francisco: Jossey-Bass.

Semler, R. (1995). *Maverick*. New York: Warner Books.

Senge, P. (1990). The fifth discipline. New York: Doubleday.

Senge, P., Roberts, C., Roth, G., Ross, R., & Smith, B. (1999). *The dance of change: The challenges to sustaining momentum in learning organizations*. New York: Doubleday/Currency.

Spitzer, Q., & Evans, R. (1997). The new business leader: Socrates with a baton. *Strategy & Leadership, 25*(5), 32–38.

Staub, J. (1991). Ask questions first to solve the right problems. *Supervisory Management, 36*(10), 7–9.

Stewart, J. (1991, June 3). Brainpower. *Fortune*, pp. 44–60.

Tichy, N. M., with Cardwell, N. (2002). *The cycle of leadership: How great leaders teach their companies to win*. New York: HarperBusiness.

Tischler, L. (2001, December). Seven strategies for successful alliances. *Fast Company*. Available online: http://www.fastcompany.com/articles/2001/12/alliances.html. Access date: March 21, 2005.

Ury, W. (1993). *Getting past no: Negotiating your way from confrontation to cooperation*. New York: Bantam Books.

Vaill, P. (1996). *Learning as a way of being: Strategies for survival in a world of permanent white water.* San Francisco: Jossey-Bass.

Welch, J. (2005) *Winning.* New York: HarperBusiness.

Wheatley, M. (2002). *Turning to one another: Simple conversations to restore hope to the future.* San Francisco: Berrett-Koehler.

Whitmore, J. (2002). *Coaching for performance: Growing people, performance and purpose.* Yarmouth, ME: Brealey.

Whitney, D., & Trosten-Bloom, A. (1998). *The power of appreciative inquiry.* San Francisco: Berrett-Koehler.

Whitney, D., Cooperrider, D., Trosten-Bloom, A., & Kaplin, B. (2002). *Encyclopedia of positive questions.* Euclid, OH: Lakeshore Communications.

Yankelovich, D. (1999). *The magic of dialogue: Transforming conflict into cooperation.* New York: Simon & Schuster.

Zuboff, S. (1989). *In the age of the smart machine: The future of work and power.* New York: Basic Books.

Acknowledgments

I am truly indebted to many people who have been instrumental in bringing this book to fruition. First, I want to thank the twenty-two leaders whose words and wisdom are found throughout this book, wonderful people who patiently answered my questions about their questioning leadership style. These leaders (listed in Resource B) offered much advice and support; all were an inspiration to me and, I am sure, will be an inspiration for thousands of readers of this book.

I especially want to thank all the folks at Jossey-Bass/Wiley, especially Rob Brandt and Alan Shrader, who guided the development of the book and helped to polish the writing.

Over the years, I have been blessed to work with and learn from a number of great leaders; leaders such as Barrie Oxtoby, Kevin Wheeler, Wayne Pace, Charles Margerison, Len Nadler, Malcolm Knowles, Reg Revans, Marilee Adams, Nissim Tal, Frank Andracchi, Pierre Gheysons, Mary Futrell, Robert Kramer, Florence Ho, Arthur Byrnes, Harry Lenderman, Steve King, Tina Sung, Nancy Stebbins, Frank Sofo, Lex Dilworth, Charles Appleby, and Ila Young.

I have learned much about leadership from my doctoral students, many of whom are now successful global leaders—Wong Wee Chwee, Antony Hii, Taebok Lee, Myoung Choi, Mary Tomasello, William Weech, Effendy Mohammed Rajab, Banu Golesorkhi, Agata Dulnik, Dan Navarro, Doug Bryant, Teo Campos, Stan Surrette, Sung Hae Kim, Marissa Wettasinghe, Somsri Siriwaiprapan, Robert Richer, Carla Bowens, Deb Waddill, Bernadette Carson, Millie Mateu, Colleen Richmond, Al McCready, Deb Gmelin, and Mabel Soh, among many others.

I wish to thank my family—my wife, Eveline, who often asks her husband *why*—and my children, Chris, Stephanie, Catherine, and Emily, who questioned their dad's wisdom, especially during their teenage years. Finally, I dedicate this book to my mother, Elaine, who encouraged me to ask questions and to always strive to keep on learning from those questions.

The Author

Michael Marquardt is professor of human resource development and program director of overseas programs at George Washington University. He also serves as president of Global Learning Associates and director of the Global Institute of Action Learning.

He has held a number of senior management, training, and marketing positions with organizations such as Grolier, American Society for Training and Development, Association Management Inc., Overseas Education Fund, TradeTec, and the U.S. Office of Personnel Management. He has trained more than seventy-five thousand managers in nearly a hundred countries since beginning his international experience in Spain in 1969. Consulting assignments have included Marriott, DuPont, Motorola, Nortel, Alcoa, Boeing, Caterpillar, United Nations Development Program, Xerox, Samsung, Brookings Institute, Nokia, Constellation, National Semiconductor, Siemens, Citicorp, Organization of American States, and Singapore Airlines, as well as the governments of Indonesia, Laos, Ethiopia, Zambia, Egypt, Kuwait, Saudi Arabia, Turkey, Russia, Jamaica, Honduras, and Swaziland.

He is the author of seventeen books and more than ninety professional articles in the fields of leadership, learning, globalization, and organizational change, including *Building the Learning Organization* (selected as Book of the Year by the Academy of HRD), *The Global Advantage*, *Action Learning in Action*, *Global Leaders for the 21st Century*, *Global Human Resource Development*, *Technology-Based Learning*, and *Global Teams*. He has been a keynote speaker at international conferences in Australia, Japan, England, the

Philippines, Malaysia, South Africa, Sweden, Singapore, and India, as well as throughout North America.

His achievements and leadership have been recognized through numerous awards, including the International Practitioner of the Year Award from the American Society for Training and Development.

He presently serves as a senior adviser for the United Nations Staff College in the areas of policy, technology, and learning systems. He is a fellow of the National Academy for Human Resource Development and a co-founder of the Asian Learning Organization Network. The International Management Centre at Oxford, England, recently awarded him an honorary Ph.D. for his work and writings in the field of action learning. He received his doctorate in human resource development from George Washington University and his master's and bachelor's degrees from Maryknoll College. He has also done graduate work at Harvard, Columbia, and the University of Virginia.

Index